RISJ *CHALLENGES*

Privacy, probity and public interest

Glenda Cooper and Stephen Whittle

REUTERS
INSTITUTE for the
STUDY of
JOURNALISM

UNIVERSITY OF
OXFORD

Contents

Executive summary

In Britain there is currently a battle engaged around the point at which freedom of information and expression meet the right to the protection of private life. Yet neither 'private life' nor 'public interest' are immutable. There have been significant changes in how both have been perceived and defined over time.

This report aims to address some of the questions over the changing nature of privacy, which private matters can be revealed by journalists in the public interest and whether the increasing use of the Human Rights Act to safeguard an individual's privacy is creating a 'chilling' effect on journalism. We have interviewed lawyers, academics, journalists, bloggers and those who have found their privacy invaded by the media—as well as those who have invaded it themselves.

New technology has been one of the main drivers of changes in perception of privacy. The internet allows private citizens to distribute photographs and information about themselves in a way unthought of only a few years ago—and which has affected the mainstream media.

This has helped foster a culture of revelation that reached its apogee this year when the *Big Brother* reality star Jade Goody continued to give interviews, be photographed and talk frankly about her cancer until she died. While many are more freely revealing intimate matters, there are those who find themselves the target of mainstream media exposés. While in the past celebrities and public figures have turned to the libel laws, now increasingly they are turning to the courts to protect their privacy—as seen in the Max Mosley case against the *News of the World* in 2008.

We need a free media that can expose wrongdoing and challenge those in power but, if the media is going to infringe privacy, it needs to take care that it is standing on the firm ground of public interest and that the means it employs to investigate are not fatally compromised either by the wrong choice of target or the manner in which the investigation is conducted. Our findings in brief are as follows:

- Most people still regard the following as essentially private: sex and sexuality; health; family life; personal correspondence and finance (except where public monies are concerned). We expect to have the highest protection of privacy around what happens in the home, in hospitals or places where people are at their most vulnerable. Children and ordinary citizens are felt to have higher rights to privacy than celebrities and public figures.

- Privacy is becoming commoditised. Celebrities are increasingly selling off selected parts of their private life through a complaisant media— while protecting other parts through the courts. Yet private citizens are increasingly putting parts of their lives on public display via the internet to seek fame or to connect with others.

- New media, especially the internet and mobile phone cameras, have rapidly altered how we can invade our own privacy—or that of others. While many regard what happens on blogs or social networking sites such as Facebook as semi-private, journalists see it as information in the public domain—and therefore fair game. The net has opened a parallel universe in which everyone is still learning to cope.

- Privacy actions have become the new libel, with many celebrities and public figures now choosing to seek redress through the Human Rights Act rather than taking their chances with libel. As such the right to privacy (Article 8) is being pitched against freedom of expression (Article 10). A succession of cases (such as *McKennitt v Ash, Lord Browne*) have seen judges look increasingly closely at how freedom of expression and personal privacy dovetail.

- The cases involving Naomi Campbell, J. K. Rowling, Princess Caroline of Monaco and Max Mosley show that the courts seem to be moving towards a much stricter interpretation of privacy when photographs are involved. It is questionable however whether there is a privacy right in one's image *per se*.

- Restrictions on resources (newspapers and broadcasters under financial restraints), time (the increasing speed of the news cycle) and perceived public indifference were all seen as more significant obstacles to investigative journalism than concerns over privacy. It is also hard to see evidence of the courts creating a 'chilling effect' on responsible journalism exercised in the public interest—particularly following landmark rulings such as *Jameel v Wall Street Journal*—although seeking to balance the freedom of expression with the competing right to privacy is never easy.

- Invasions of privacy 'in the public interest' are justified by some journalists (primarily the editor of the *Daily Mail*, Paul Dacre) as a moral venture. Journalists frequently cite hypocrisy on the part of a public figure or their status as a 'role model' in order to validate such invasions. We argue that it is hard to prove a connection between private behaviour and public actions. The person who believes in flying saucers or is conducting a sado-masochistic relationship may be a council officer or a department store manager. If, in an investigation, links are shown to exist between the public and the private, then the latter is a legitimate area of inquiry. But there is no prima facie public interest in ET believers, or in sado-masochists.

- Any approach which recognises that the private space is to be, in principle, protected will run the risk of missing concealed scandals which bear on public life—for example, the David Blunkett nanny scandal. But to argue from this that all potentially compromising private relationships must therefore be investigated is not a reasonable posture. There is a greater public interest in the protection of private life: and that interest must tolerate the occasional missed misdemeanour.

In practical terms, media investigations have to be proportionate to what is being investigated and clearly targeted. That implies:
- a clear sense of what the public interest justification might be;
- the possession of some justifying evidence to take an investigation forward so that it is not a 'fishing expedition';
- the minimum amount of deception to achieve it;
- very clear rules about when secret recording takes place;
- a clear set of authorisations from within the editorial line management chain;
- a robust rationale for what is eventually put into the public domain and how.

Introduction

In July 2008, a case was decided in the High Court in London which encapsulated some of the contemporary tensions between private and public life. Max Mosley, president of the Formula One association, successfully sued the *News of the World* for breaching his privacy in the way in which it reported a sado-masochistic orgy in which he had been involved.

Since this case is a central event in our argument, we should begin with a short account of it. Max Mosley, son of Sir Oswald the former leader of the British Union of Fascists, and president of the Federation Internationale de l'Automobile which oversees Formula One racing, was revealed, in March 2008 by the *News of the World*, to have taken part in sado-masochistic sex games with five prostitutes, in a context which the newspaper claimed included Nazi role-playing.

Mosley admitted the event but denied the context: and in July 2008, he won a High Court case against the *NoW* on the grounds of invasion of privacy. Mr Justice Eady, the judge, found there to be no 'suggestion that the participants mocked the victims of the Holocaust'.[1]

At the heart of the case which caused such a furore, and of others which we will cite, lie two issues. First, what is the nature of private life, and what behaviour warrants intrusion into it by the news media? And second, what is the nature of the public interest, how far is it consonant with or different from what interests the public—and how broadly should it be now defined?

These two notions, private life and the public interest, are central

[1] L. Holmwood and C. Fitzsimmons, 'Max Mosley Wins £60,000 in Privacy Case', *Guardian*, 24 July 2008: www.guardian.co.uk/uk/2008/jul/24/mosley.privacy

dilemmas for the practice of contemporary journalism. They have been so for a long time—for at least a century and a half, since reporting techniques that we would recognize as modern began to be developed—but the dilemmas are sharper now, and can only become more so, for reasons we will examine.

These reasons, briefly, include:
- the changing nature of the law, especially on privacy;
- the ubiquity of the internet, and its ability to redefine privacy;
- the increasing importance of social networking, and the creation of so-called 'declarative lifestyles', in the virtual world;
- the changing priorities of the news media, especially at a time when they are afflicted by a loss of revenue and cutbacks in many areas;
- the growth in the importance of celebrities of all kinds, often presented—or who present themselves—as role models, especially to the young, and who use slices of their private lives for sale as commodities which the media use as a justification for further intrusion;
- the spread of that celebrity culture to non-celebrities via reality shows, and their exploitation of what would have previously been regarded as private, even intimate, events and moments.

In a fine synopsis of present trends, Emily Bell, director of digital content for Guardian News and Media, has written that:

> *It has never been easier to discover the whereabouts, dealings and behaviour of any individual. We live in times when privacy has to be actively sought rather than occurring as a matter of course, where half the population seems happy to share their lives with the public—photos, details, blogs—and where you do not have to be very nosy before you find yourself in possession of 'too much information'. The internet is an awesome tool that allows us to pick over the contemporary alongside the past, and to identify minute details from recorded conversations, examining them for inconsistencies and hidden meaning. Blogs and other media outlets, meanwhile, serve to push a story along in the dog days of slow news. If you are a public figure with something to hide it is a relentlessly miserable place to be.*[2]

---

[2] E. Bell, 'The Guilty should Beware the Black Arts of the Bloggers', *Guardian*, 10 July 2006: www.guardian.co.uk/media/2006/jul/10/mondaymediasection.comment

More and more, we see a battle engaged around the point at which freedom of information and expression meets the right to the protection of private life. Neither 'private life' nor 'public interest' are immutable. There have been significant changes in how both have been perceived and defined over time: the present is only distinguished by the speed of the contemporary changes.

The contemporary view of privacy, its place in an open but humane society, and what justifies its exposure to the public space, presents us with a series of paradoxes and challenges. Our focus here is on privacy and the media but it cannot ignore the social, cultural, legal and regulatory framework in which that interaction takes place.

We therefore seek to understand the mixed views and behaviours people exhibit when it comes to their private lives; how and why journalists act as they do when their search for a story causes them to infringe privacy; the way in which judges, regulators and politicians frame their response; and ask what is the public interest that justifies intrusion.

As we proceeded, we heard from many people that the 'public interest' is a slippery notion to define: some of our respondents said it was impossible, others that it was better not to define it, since a lack of a firm definition means greater flexibility all round, especially for journalists.

Our belief is that isn't so—especially for journalism. A robust approach to what constitutes the public interest, which we attempt here, is both an affirmation of, and a protection for, the kind of journalism that free societies need, and non-free societies aspire to.

1. Privacy in context

On 30 January 2001, a beautiful young woman left a building in Chelsea, talked to some friends and walked along the street. She was photographed as she did so.

There was nothing particularly striking about the image itself; it could have been any woman photographed in any street. But the *Daily Mirror*'s decision to publish that picture of the supermodel Naomi Campbell outside a Narcotics Anonymous meeting proved to be one of the most important developments in the law relating to privacy in the last ten years.

Campbell alleged that the photographs published of her exit from Narcotics Anonymous was a breach of her privacy, and took the *Mirror* to court. She lost to the paper in the Appeal Court, but on the final appeal, to the Lords, she won a 3–2 verdict that her privacy was invaded. The size of the damages—£3,500, probably little more than the cost of a shopping expedition for her—showed that the Lords did not rate the distress the invasion caused as very high: but the *Mirror* got a legal bill estimated at over £1m. The *Mirror* had run a story about the model's alleged drug addiction—and had published the photograph to give credence to the story. Though the Lords' majority chose to protect her private life, Lord Hoffman, one of the two dissenters from the majority verdict, said after the case that 'from a journalistic point of view, photographs are an essential part of the story. The picture carried the message, more strongly than anything in the text alone, that the *Mirror*'s story was true.'[3]

Six months before Campbell was pictured walking out of that building on the King's Road, west London, an equally important development in our understanding of privacy took place in east London. On 14 July 2000,

[3] *Campbell v MGN Ltd* [2004] UKHL (6 May 2004), para. 77: w.bailii.org/uk/cases/UKHL/2004/22.html

several strangers entered a house, where they would later run around naked and daubed in paint for the benefit of a television audience.

In their way, Nichola Holt, Craig Phillips and the other contestants taking part in the first series of *Big Brother* broadcast on Channel 4 in 2000, were helping to redefine the twenty-first-century approach to privacy. As Mark Frith, former editor of *heat* magazine puts it: 'This was a new generation … who had no problems living their lives publicly, with every aspect of their lives on show. For them it made total sense … and it was what gave them their career.'[4]

So while public figures who have become famous now often go to greater and greater lengths to ensure their lives remain private, this contrasts with private citizens who wish to become famous or at least better known, who are putting their lives on public display, giving up their privacy to connect with strangers and acquire some fame. As Martin Soames, a media lawyer at Best & Soames has put it, private information:

> has become a commodity—if you're an ordinary person it is something that you use like Pokémon cards, to swap with other people. But at the other end of the scale, for the rich and famous, it is a different kind of commodity, something that's valuable through its scarcity and their control of it.[5]

A third development has ensured that keeping a secret is harder, and creating notoriety is much easier. The relevant date for that could be 15 September 1997, when Larry Page and Sergey Brin first registered the search engine google.com. Arguably it could be pushed further back—to 25 December 1990, when British scientist Tim Berners-Lee implemented the first successful communication between a hypertext client and server via the internet thus paving the way for the World Wide Web. Internet technology has made it much easier to obtain, store and disseminate what in the past could have remained private information, or been confined to a small number of those in the know.

Privacy has been commoditised. On the one hand individuals now have the possibility to profit from the manipulation of their privacy—whether by allowing it to be displayed in carefully organised and packaged slices, as celebrities of all kinds do; or by offering it up on the altar of the public gaze, as those wishing to be famous, or only to 'connect', as *Big Brother* demonstrates. On the other, unauthorised or intrusive exposure is now a

---

[4] Phone interview, 10 Sept. 2008.
[5] J. Robins, 'Which Parts of Your Life are Really Private?', *Guardian*, 17 Sept. 2007: www.guardian.co.uk/media/2007/sep/17/pressandpublishing.law

bigger issue than in the past—both financially (for the celebrity) and legally (for the courts).

Courts are taking a greater role in deciding the point at which privacy requires protection, even if the person involved is a 24-carat celebrity like Campbell. In this chapter, we set out some basics of modern privacy, largely as the news media see it in practice. We want to see

- how it has been and is now defined;
- to whom the right to privacy is extended;
- when it takes precedence over exposure;
- where, if anywhere, privacy is deemed to be inviolable.

What is privacy?

In 1890, in the first decades of a genuinely mass (and intrusive) news media, the US Supreme Court Justice, Louis Brandeis, famously described privacy as 'the right to be left alone'.[6] Robert Ellis Smith, editor of the *Privacy Journal*, is more detailed: he suggests that privacy is 'the desire by each of us for physical space where we can be free of interruption, intrusion, embarrassment, or accountability and the attempt to control the time and manner of disclosures of personal information about ourselves'.[7]

As Peter Bradwell and Niamh Gallagher, writing in the Demos publication *UK Confidential* claim:

> *Privacy still matters because it provides the space to withdraw from the gaze of others and to rest from the need to perform socially. Moreover it matters politically and democratically because it is intimately connected with how we are seen, represented and treated by the people, organisations and institutions that hold influence and power over us.*[8]

Intrusions on privacy by journalists are as old as the press, in one form or another: but contemporary debates are conveniently dated from the late 1980s, as complaints grew over a more aggressive journalistic style. In 1989, the Calcutt Committee was set up by the Government to investigate privacy and press behaviour, following the comment from the

---

[6] J. Michael, *Privacy and Human Rights* (UNESCO, 1994), 1. As quoted by Privacy International.
[7] R. Ellis Smith, *Ben Franklin's Web Site* (Sheridan Books, 2000), 6. Also quoted by Privacy International.
[8] Samuel Warren and Louis Brandeis, 'The Right to Privacy', *Harvard Law Review*, 4 (1890), 193–220.

Conservative minister David Mellor that the 'sacred cow' of press freedom should be challenged, since newspapers were 'drinking in the last chance saloon'. Its report, published in June 1990, recommended the establishment of a voluntary body which would seek to enforce compliance with a set of rules on ethical standards, above all on the approach taken to privacy. This was the Press Complaints Commission, which superseded the Press Council. Calcutt produced a potential legal definition: privacy is 'the right of the individual to be protected against intrusion into his personal life or affairs, or those of his family, by direct physical means, or by publication of information'.[9]

It is worth remembering that the Calcutt Committee came into being as the result of a growing unease following a number of press scandals around intrusion in the 1970s and 1980s. People in the public eye, from the Queen to entertainers such as the chat show host Russell Harty, the singer Elton John and the actor Gorden Kaye, together with a number of politicians, had found themselves at the wrong end of a lens or a prying eye. Kaye, well known for his role as Rene Artois in the comedy series *'Allo 'Allo*, had sustained serious head injuries in a car accident in January 1990: while in hospital, he was 'interviewed' by the *Sunday Sport* journalist Roger Ordish. He failed in his bid to stop the *Sunday Sport* publishing the 'interview': Lord Justice Glidewell said in his judgment that

> *If ever a person has a right to be let alone by strangers with no public interest to pursue, it must surely be when he lies in hospital recovering from brain surgery and in no more than partial command of his faculties. It is this invasion of his privacy which underlies the plaintiff's complaint. Yet it alone, however gross, does not entitle him to relief in English law.*[10]

According to media commentator Roy Greenslade, the age of decency and deference that had marked the 1920s and the 1930s had become, from the 1940s onwards, the age of irreverence, suspicion and intrusion. Greenslade has described the post-war period as opening the doors to a greater suspicion of what the 'toffs' might be up to, and a greater readiness to question their decisions. It led to more challenging journalism—but also a greater readiness to invade privacy. It was a tendency which accelerated

---

[9] *Report of the Committee on Privacy and Related Matters* (Cm. 1102, HMSO, 1990), 7.
[10] *10 Kaye v Robertson* [1991] FSR 62. It can be found at
http://216.239.59.104/search?q=cache:fMPVr3_TGDoJ:www.a-level-law.com/caselibrary/
KAYE%2520v%2520ROBERTSON%2520%255B1991%255D%2520FSR%252062%2520-
%2520CA.doc+%22gorden+kaye%22+and+%22sunday+sport%22&hl=en&ct=clnk&cd=7&client=safari

through the 1970s and 1980s, to what he has called a kind of 'Wild West moment',[11] after which almost anything went. This 'free for all' culminated in the creation of the Press Complaints Commission in 1990 as mentioned earlier, to replace a Press Council that was seen as ineffectual.

The Calcutt Report made clear that the new Commission would have eighteen months to demonstrate 'that non-statutory self-regulation can be made to work effectively. This is a stiff test for the press. If it fails, we recommend that a statutory system for handling complaints should be introduced.'[12]

A statutory system in the form of a privacy law has never yet been implemented, despite repeated threats. But since then, there have been significant shifts in how privacy is dealt with. First, as many of the journalists we interviewed maintained, celebrities and public figures are still regarded as 'fair game' if they have already sought any kind of publicity. It is seen, by journalists, as an open question as to whether they have the right to some life beyond the lens, and whether or not they have a say in where those boundaries are set.

Second, there is a changing idea of what privacy is, and where its boundaries lie: is it, as Mark Frith argues 'what happens behind closed doors'[13] or can it encompass walking down a public street—as both Naomi Campbell, and the author of Harry Potter books, J. K. Rowling, have argued in court?[14] Part of this is a cultural challenge; and in a globalised world, different ideas collide. As Rosen argues in *UK Confidential*:

> *Europeans are far more sensitive than Americans about disclosing financial information, steeped as they are in the aristocratic tradition that respectable people don't discuss money in public. Why is it that French people won't talk about their salaries but will take off their bikini tops?*[15]

The third shift—and a massive one—has been technological. Discussions of privacy in the past have focused on the mainstream media; now, they more often concern the ability of journalists—and increasingly of 'citizen journalists' as well as those who wish to invade their own privacy—to put material on the net without control or redress. The real

[11] Interview, London, 9 Oct. 2008.
[12] From the history of the Press Complaints Commission: www.pcc.org.uk/about/history.html
[13] Phone interview, 10 Sept. 2008.
[14] A. Singh, 'J. K. Rowling Wins Privacy Case over Son's Photos', *Daily Telegraph*, 8 May 2008: www.telegraph.co.uk/news/uknews/1936471/JK-Rowling-wins-privacy-case-over-son's-photos.html
[15] Edwards and Fieschi, *UK Confidential*, 144.

challenges are now seen as coming from the technology which alters how we can invade our own privacy by publicising our own lives—or that of others—via blogs, or through the increasing use of mobile phone cameras. For example, *heat* magazine's 'Spotted' and 'Snapped' pages encourage readers to send in sightings or photographs of celebrities they've come across, while on the Gawker website (www.gawker.com), people email in real time to say where and when they have spotted celebrities around New York.

These new media have also made information far more accessible; in the past, mainstream media reports may have had limited circulation, and years after the event were only to be found tucked away in mouldering newspaper libraries or hidden reels of film. But the advent of digital technology, the increasing use of online archives and the development of search engines like the market leader, Google, mean that it is extremely easy to dig out information on anyone rapidly, even years after an original report. On the first meeting between one of us and Rachel North, a survivor of the 7/7 bombings in London who began a blog after the event, she was able to say:

> *I know where you went to school, where you've worked, where you've worked abroad, that you like modern novels, that you use your mobile phone and feel lost without it, that you're married. I found that all out in ten minutes.*[16]

Who has a right to privacy?

For this study, we have interviewed journalists, academics, lawyers and bloggers about their views on privacy. The one question that came up time and again was *who* has the right to privacy. For most of the journalists, the question came down simply to whether someone had put their life in any way into the public domain, whether through seeking national public office or by being elected a local carnival queen. There was generally a sliding scale. Politicians came out at the top, but journalists argue that any appearance in, or cooperation with, the media could lay you open to investigation. As David Leigh, the veteran investigative reporter for the *Guardian* put it: 'A lot more of your life is fair game if you put yourself in the public arena.'[17]

[16] Interview, London, 28 July 2008.
[17] Interview, London, 4 Nov. 2008.

Chris Loweth, head of legal compliance at Channel Five, significantly refines Leigh's position. He says he always asks the question: 'Is he or she a public figure *whose public position justifies the intervention?*'[18] (He says he would also ask the existential question of the producer working on the story: 'how would you feel if this were *you*?') David Henshaw of Hard Cash productions suggested a further test: 'What does this person *represent*?'[19]

The BBC, too, seeks to calibrate exposure of public people according to significance—while admitting this calibration would differ according to which of the many BBC channels was involved. Kevin Marsh, Editor of the BBC's College of Journalism, says:

> *We would take the view that a CEO of a major energy multinational has to expect some level of intrusion. We think it would be reasonable to doorstep Sir Thingy Thingy in charge of a public body whereas we would not think it would be reasonable to doorstep Joe Bloggs of 26 Acacia Avenue. By and large, celebrity is not the thing that does it. Radio 1 and 1Xtra might see it differently as celebs are very important [to them] … These people have a deal with the public, we make you famous and in return you have to give us some access to your lives. But as you go away from the Radio 1 end of things—News 24, Radio 4—it matters less and less.*[20]

Reasons commonly given by journalists for a breach of privacy

Hypocrisy. If a public figure's private life contradicts their public pronouncements (e.g. a politician with a secret sexual life who sells himself on a 'family values platform; an actor who denounces drugs while indulging in private).

Public accountability. Again if private life compromises a public figure's ability to carry out their duties (e.g. a businessman who does favours involving company money for a secret lover).

'The Deal'/Faustian pact. Celebrities and public figures do a deal with the media to highlight their image and raise their profile. Therefore if they sell part of their private lives, they should not have the right to veto other parts of it from being exposed.

'Fair game'. By agreeing to being in the public eye at all, public figures have sacrificed their right to privacy.

The 'role model' argument. Celebrities and public figures have become role models, therefore we have the right to know about details about their private lives.

The Dacre argument: Shaming is vital to uphold morality and public standards of decency. If mass circulation papers can't report scandal it will mean a loss of circulation and that has implications for democracy.

(Source: interviews for report)

---

[18] Interview, London, 4 Nov. 2008.
[19] Interview, London, 17 July 2008.

[20] Interview, London, 24 Sept. 2008.

In the high-profile case of Max Mosley, the justification used by the *News of the World* for its investigation drew heavily both on the perceived importance of Mosley's role, and on the fact that he was elected to it. Tom Crone, legal manager at News International, argued that, although not well known, Mosley's job justified putting him in the spotlight:

> *Mosley was elected … he was elected five times since 1991 as head of the FIA (Federation Internationale de l'Automobile), a global organization with effectively 125m members—which probably makes it bigger than the American electorate. He is elected by all these people through their national representatives. And amongst its powers the FIA runs motorsport around the world, if you just took Formula One … we say that puts him absolutely four-square as an important public figure. He may not be terribly well-known as a name, but he is a big-time public figure.*[21]

Political bloggers are also comfortable with the idea that, if someone has put himself or herself into the public domain, then they can expect to have their private life scrutinised. Guido Fawkes (real name Paul Staines and author of www.order-order.com) said: 'My view can be summed up as essentially believing that public figures implicitly consent to public scrutiny. If you want privacy, stay a private person.'[22] The Conservative activist and blogger Iain Dale (author of *Iain Dale's Diary*) confirmed that these were the well-known rules of the game—'Most politicians understand this'—but added:

> *Most of them are not famous until they are in their 40s and who in their 40s has done nothing that they wouldn't mind appearing in newspapers? That puts a lot of people going off into political and public life. Why put your family through that agony? We are missing out whole range of people—we'll never have another Churchill or Lloyd George—imagine them today. We are getting little personalities with little experience of life—and I'm not sure politics is the better for it.*[23]

The issue of who has the right to privacy is further complicated by the practice of the deals struck between powerful agents/management on the

---

[21] Interview, London, 13 Aug. 2008.
[22] Personal communication, 10 July 2008.
[23] Interview, London, 2 Sept. 2008.

one hand and media—eager for access to celebrities—on the other. These are deals designed to ensure that many less flattering stories about the famous are never published.

In an interview to publicise his authorised biography, the publicist Max Clifford was clear about the 'deals' struck. These are not always simply straightforward negotiations for the highest amount of money: they can also be *quid pro quo* deals—one sensational account offered to get another story in (or keep another story out of) the tabloids. As Clifford said:

> *With David Beckham [when he had an affair with his personal assistant] it was money. A lot of money. With Jude Law [when he had an affair with his children's nanny] I was able to use that to do all sorts of deals for other clients of mine. I could say to an editor, I'll give you this story if you help publicise something else I'm involved with.*[24]

The deal culture has spawned its own corrective: it was, avowedly, to counter it that the gossip website Popbitch was set up by journalists Neil Stevenson and Camilla Wright eight years ago. It is still run out of a small office in Soho and consists of a weekly newsletter sent to around 370,000 people plus a scabrous message forum in which celebrities are regularly ridiculed and titbits of information shared. Wright said that the idea behind it was:

> *a way of getting information out, information that was not filtered by publicists or the rich and famous, and therefore it was a way for people to talk about what was going on with the world. We are talking about the behaviour of pop stars—so I don't think that can be said to be in the public interest, although it is something the public is interested in. … But a lot of celebrities are multimillion brands so if they are pushing out lies to maintain their contracts or an image that gives them money then pointing out hypocrisy is a good thing to do … we were pushing against the culture that rich and famous people use the media to institutionalise lying to the public, and making people aware how that is going on.*[25]

[24] J. Preston, 'Max Clifford Exposed!', *Daily Telegraph,* 27 Sept. 2005:
www.telegraph.co.uk/arts/main.jhtml?xml=/arts/2005/09/27/boclifford25.xml
[25] Interview, London, 7 Oct. 2008.

Wright says that she currently has around 200–500 sources of which 50–100 provide almost half of all her stories: journalists who pass on information they cannot print themselves; publicists; celebrity hairdressers, stylists or make-up artists who have been treated badly; limo drivers and lawyers who, Wright says, 'are far less discreet than you might imagine'.

Celebrities can generally manage their public profile: private citizens who become unexpected public figures through reality shows or through blogging generally cannot, if and when they become sucked into a media frenzy. For some bloggers it comes as shock that, if they are successful, they are seen as 'fair game' for investigation by other internet users or the mainstream media.

Rachel North—the woman who had told us she knew many private details about us before we met—had survived a violent rape in July 2002, then found herself in the underground train bombed in July 2005. She began a much-read blog soon afterwards. She says:

I honestly thought the only people reading [my blog] would be parents, family, friends and other survivors. I was extremely naive and brutally honest on that blog. I can't be now, three years on. I thought I was anonymous, no one knew what I looked like, no one knew my name, and I felt protected by the anonymity of it all.[26]

Zoe Margolis, a former assistant film director and author of the sexually explicit *Girl With A One Track Mind* blog which she published under the pseudonym Abby Lee, had taken careful precautions to ensure that she was not named when a book was published from her online diary. She had always maintained her *nom de plume* and the number of people who knew her true identity could be counted on one hand. So she felt completely powerless when the *Sunday Times* revealed her name:

When it happened I felt like my world collapsed. A friend said later he thought I was having a breakdown. I was sleeping three, four hours a night. I was anxious, I became agoraphobic, couldn't talk on the phone and didn't know what I was going to do as I hadn't earned enough from the book deal to retire. How was I going to pay my rent? I had been working on Harry Potter 5 but was even banned from the cast and crew screening a year later.

[26] Interview, London, 28 July 2008.

I'm a nobody, I had nothing of interest to say, I'd not shagged any celebrities or politicians and they still blackmailed me to talk to them … So now whenever I see 'my side of the story'—drink or drugs—I think they [celebrities] have been pushed into it.[27]

Former *heat* editor Mark Frith, however, was convinced that most of those who had come into the public domain via reality shows were usually clear about the deal that had been done, and would continue to reveal details about their private lives in order to stay in the public domain. When asked whether people would refuse to answer personal questions, his response was: 'That would happen very rarely and if so, they would usually duck out of public life altogether … They put their lives on show and they were comfortable to be seen in that way subsequently.'[28] His justification was that essentially such people became a form of 'role model'. In an increasingly fragmented society, he believes, reality stars and celebrities have taken the place of previous figures of authority such as family members, religious figures, and politicians in formulating and dictating the way one should behave in life.[29] The 'journey' which the most successful reality TV stars articulate—with, commonly, an account of a difficult start in life, self-realisation through tasks they set themselves, to eventual triumph—functions as a modern day *Pilgrim's Progress*.

Figures such as the late Jade Goody of *Big Brother*, whose battle with cervical cancer became well-documented or Sharon Osbourne of *The Osbournes*, Frith claimed, performed a valuable service by talking about intimate areas of their life.

We are living through times where people want reassurance, life lessons and advice and we want case studies and examples. So when Sharon Osbourne talks in her autobiography about her health problems and her family, people read that to learn how to deal with similar things.[30]

---

[27] Interview, London, 7 Aug. 2008.
[28] Phone interview, London, 10 Sept. 2008.
[29] Committee on Standards of Conduct in Public Life, *Third National Survey of Public Attitudes on Standards of Conduct in Public Life* (2008). The full report can be found at: www.public-standards.org.uk/Library/SOPA_bookmarked.pdf. This Mori poll published in Nov. 2008 found that only 26% trusted MPs to tell the truth, and 27% trusted government ministers. It is perhaps worth noting that the least likely of the 17 professions mentioned to be perceived to tell the truth is the tabloid journalist.
[30] Phone interview, London, 10 Sept. 2008.

The exception to this loosening of privacy is for those under 16. There does seem to be a consensus that children are increasingly off-limits. The approach taken by the media, as well as the judgments of regulators and the courts, indicate that the rules are tighter. Chris Loweth, head of legal compliance at Channel Five, says that Ofcom is now 'much tougher' around children and young people, although he believes they are confusing the obligation to protect under 18s and rights to privacy.[31]

For example, last year Ofcom found against Channel 4 filming a young person known as Child K during a documentary about child smokers. Child K had said he was 16 but was in fact 14: at the same time, by asking K at what age he started smoking, Ofcom ruled that the programme makers had asked him questions of a personal nature which required consent from his mother despite the public interest argument about child smoking.[32]

Newspapers have also become much more cautious about what they print about children. An example: in a recent newspaper interview, a celebrity chef talked for the first time about being awarded custody of his children. Though he spoke freely, the newspaper was reluctant to reproduce the details—some of which had already been put in the public domain—because of fears over breaching the PCC code.[33]

The investigative journalist Nick Davies argues that there can be occasions that justify a breach of the code. He gave the example of interviewing children in care in Nottingham who were working as prostitutes:

> *I wrote a book about poverty and the kick-off for that was meeting two boys in a fairground in Nottingham aged 10 or 11 who were clearly selling their bodies to passers-by. I started talking to them—they were in care—and arranged to meet them. The following day, I was sitting with them in a square and a social worker walked by, recognised them and realised they were talking to a journalist … got on to the Guardian and got very heavy. And I resisted that. There are rules that you can't interview children without parents' consent and the children's home is in loco parentis. But part of the story was that most of the underage boys and girls working as prostitutes in Nottingham were in children's homes and most of those homes either couldn't be bothered to stop*

[31] Interview, London, 17 July 2008.
[32] Ofcom Broadcast Bulletin 106 (Apr. 2008): www.ofcom.org.uk/tv/obb/prog_cb/obb106/bb106.pdf
[33] Personal communication.

them or were unable to stop them. That's important and needs to be said and I thought it was important to not surrender the story to those who were at fault. There is a privacy issue—but I would deal with that by not identifying [the children].[34]

Davies's point is an important one for journalists: it expresses a widely held view in the profession that a journalist should have the moral right to decide whether bending or breaking otherwise reasonable rules is legitimate in pursuit of a higher goal—the revelation of a scandal. (Davies himself refers to this as the 'Anne Frank rule': that is, that although it is generally the right thing to do to tell the truth, there are circumstances where the moral position is to lie fluently—using the example of Wehrmacht soldiers asking the whereabouts of the Frank family, in hiding in Amsterdam.)

Many journalists also believe that, while politicians' children may have a right to a private life, this is overruled when private activity sits against public statements. Thus the case of Euan Blair found drunk in Leicester Square, or Will Straw selling drugs were justified as stories, given Tony Blair's recent pronouncements on drunks being marched to cashpoints, and Jack Straw as Home Secretary taking a tough line on drugs. At least one judge agrees: 'Children', says Mr Justice Eady, 'in those circumstances are fair game, even if it's cruel.'[35]

When should privacy prevail?

The traditional human rights approach—as in the Universal Declaration of Human Rights—sees family, correspondence and finance as key elements to protect from intrusion. Our interviewees also listed health and sex. As Tom Crone of News International put it:

It would take a very large public interest to override the confidentiality of medical records, personal financial records compared with company ones, and a particularly large public interest to override what we would call 'normal sexual activity'.[36]

[34] Interview, Lewes, 13 Aug. 2008.
[35] Interview, London, 17 Jan. 2008.
[36] Interview, London, 10 Sept. 2008.

Sex

This issue at first glance might seem straightforward: sexual intimacy is something that belongs to our most private expression of need and affection. For most of us, it is the most personal activity. What real public interest is there in knowing what people get up to in the privacy of their own bedrooms—or even other people's? (Although it is perhaps worth remembering that in the 2002 case of *Theakston v MGN*—the *Top of the Pops* presenter Jamie Theakston's action against the *Sunday People*—Mr Justice Ouseley decided that in his view a brothel could not be termed a 'private place'.[37])

The former Information Commissioner, Richard Thomas, says that

> *A journalist who bought information on sexual activities would be hard-pressed to justify it: one, sex is only recorded on health and medical files; two, it is treated as sensitive data; and three, it is not often that sexual activity needs to be exposed in the public interest. A 'family values' politician who has a mistress is fair game, but you can't obtain private information to prove this.*[38]

A related issue is that of *sexuality*; is it right to refer to or reveal someone's sexual orientation if they are gay? Ten years ago *The Sun* declared it would no longer out people unless there was 'an overwhelming public interest' (this decision followed a story three days earlier entitled: 'Tell Us the Truth Tony: Are We Being Run by a Gay Mafia?'[39] and exposés on the politicians Nick Brown and Peter Mandelson).

Does this mean that there are no more brutal outings by the press? Not quite: what is now more common is a different approach. Evidence of gay sexual behaviour is collected, and the paper then invites the subject to open his/her heart to its readers—and thus out themselves. For example, when Will Young won the reality show *Pop Idol* in 2002 he decided to out himself in the *News of the World*, with the cryptic remark: 'Some other media pressure has led me to talk about my private life.' Five newspapers had contacted the publicist Max Clifford in the belief he had access to a former lover of Young's. After the *Mail on Sunday* started investigating Young's past, lawyers for his management company 19 cited Young's right to privacy under the PCC code and the Human Rights Act: but then abandoned the high road in favour of the lower road, taken by Young's

---

[37] J. Coad, 'Sex and Privacy: *Theakston v MGN Ltd*', *Swan Turton ebulletin*, 19 Feb 2002: www.swanturton.com/ebulletins/archive/JKCSexandprivacy.aspx

[38] Interview, London, 8 Feb. 2008.

[39] Leading article, *The Sun*, 9 Nov. 1998.

public relations company, of managing the announcement by going to the papers instead.[40] Another example is Stephen Gately, of the boy band Boyzone who ended up declaring his sexuality on the front page of *The Sun* under the 'world exclusive' headline: 'Boyzone Stephen: I'm Gay and I'm in Love'[41]—after fearing that a former member of Boyzone's security was about to sell the story. Gately's manager Louis Walsh later commented that Gately had 'been forced out by the *Sun*'[42]—a claim *The Sun* then vehemently denied.

For many broadsheets and broadcasters, this approach is seen as bullying and homophobic. Camilla Wright of Popbitch says that she would never, for example, out a gay footballer, adding: 'I think there's enough homophobic press out there; I don't think we would do that till society changes'.[43] (She makes a distinction between pop music, where to be gay is acceptable, she believes, and Hollywood and sport, where it is not.)

David Leigh of the *Guardian* says, however, that it is difficult to make hard and fast rules. Using the example of Lord Mandelson, who has been the subject of frequent innuendo about his sexuality, Leigh says that there is an argument that such homophobic commentary is a price we may have to pay. Leigh—one of the few remaining fulltime investigative reporters, with a string of successful revelations to his credit—reveals himself as a fundamentalist on this question:

> *People are entitled to know whom Peter Mandelson is sleeping with, if only on the grounds of pillow talk—just as if you should know whom a heterosexual person is married to, so that you can see if they are getting preferential treatment because of who their partner is. So you should make clear who Mandelson's partner is and if they are male, so be it. On the other hand the Daily Mail uses this to make homophobic intrusions into Mandelson's private life all the time which is horrid and morally unjustified. ... [But] philosophically my starting point has always been liberty is indivisible so we probably have to put up with a lot of bad stuff in the name of free speech. So the Sun and the News of the World are the price we pay for liberty.*[44]

---

[40] S. Boggan, 'A Pop Idol, a Rumour, and Why He Felt He Had to Come Out', *Independent,* 11 Mar. 2002: www.independent.co.uk/arts-entertainment/music/news/a-pop-idol-a-rumour-and-why-he-felt-he-had-to-come-out-653589.html

[41] R. Singh, 'Boyzone Stephen: I'm Gay and I'm in Love', *The Sun*, 16 June 1999.

[42] N. Horan, 'Louis "Mightn't Have Picked" Gay Gately', *Irish Times*, 23 Nov. 2008: www.independent.ie/entertainment/news-gossip/louis-mightnt-have-picked-gay-gately-1550151.html

[43] Interview, London, 7 Oct. 2008.

[44] Interview, London, 4 Nov. 2008.

Though Leigh differs sharply from many of the practices of the tabloid press, his approach to sexual revelations is similar to theirs. He says that, while the broadsheets are usually reluctant to cover sexual scandals because they don't see a public interest justification, it is difficult to make hard and fast rules. He argues that some of his colleagues had been 'naïve' in dismissing all cases as grubby tabloid fare: his argument reveals that he believes sexual relations between people of differing political views may, prima facie, be an expression of hypocrisy. He says:

> *The classic was David Blunkett carrying on with Kimberly Fortier where the first reaction in the Guardian was 'oh this isn't in the public interest; who he has sex with is his business'. That turned out to be wrong because not only was he sleeping with someone of violently different political persuasion which raises questions of hypocrisy but he was allegedly doing favours for her nanny and whatever because he was smitten with her. Then there were a whole set of issues over whether he'd fathered her child. So that first impulse to say 'leave it alone' was mistaken.*
>
> *This isn't a new problem. I had an identical problem 30 years ago trying to investigate Jeremy Thorpe in 1979 when he was accused of conspiring to kill his gay lover. When we looked into it, people at the Guardian were very reluctant to support our investigation because they thought it was homophobic and he was being persecuted because he was gay. Once again, this initial stance was wrong because it turned out he was hiring hitmen which put it firmly into a public arena. So that rather naïve impulse that it was all about his private life was dumb.*[45]

Health

If sex has been a key ingredient of journalism for decades, health has usually been treated as more of a taboo, especially since the Naomi Campbell case. Of the adjudicated complaints for the Press Complaints Commission between September 2007 and September 2008,[46] only three were related to Article 3 of the code on rights to privacy on health; and in these cases, the breach of the code related more to carelessness, rather than deliberately setting out to reveal someone's health status without consent.

---

[45] Interview, London, 4 Nov. 2008.
[46] See the PCC website for details www.pcc.org.uk/cases/adjudicated.html

The Press Complaints Commission, established after the publication of the Calcutt Report in 1990, is appointed and funded by the newspaper industry. Complainants offended by material in a newspaper which pertains to them can address themselves to the PCC for redress—which takes the form of a censure and the publication of an apology.

The preamble to the Code

All members of the press have a duty to maintain the highest professional standards. The Code, which includes this preamble and the public interest exceptions below, sets the benchmark for those ethical standards, protecting both the rights of the individual and the public's right to know. It is the cornerstone of the system of self-regulation to which the industry has made a binding commitment.

It is essential that an agreed code be honoured not only to the letter but in the full spirit. It should not be interpreted so narrowly as to compromise its commitment to respect the rights of the individual, nor so broadly that it constitutes an unnecessary interference with freedom of expression or prevents publication in the public interest.

It is the responsibility of editors and publishers to apply the Code to editorial material in both printed and online versions of publications. They should take care to ensure it is observed rigorously by all editorial staff and external contributors, including non-journalists, in printed and online versions of publications. Editors should co-operate swiftly with the PCC in the resolution of complaints. Any publication judged to have breached the Code must print the adjudication in full and with due prominence, including headline reference to the PCC.

Articles 1–3 of the Code

1. Accuracy

The Press must take care not to publish inaccurate, misleading or distorted information, including pictures.

2. Opportunity to reply

A fair opportunity for reply to inaccuracies must be given when reasonably called for.

3. Privacy

i) Everyone is entitled to respect for his or her private and family life, home, health and correspondence, including digital communications. Editors will be expected to justify intrusions into any individual's private life without consent.

ii) It is unacceptable to photograph individuals in a private place without their consent.

Note—Private places are public or private property where there is a reasonable expectation of privacy.

On the public interest

1. The public interest includes, but is not confined to:

i) Detecting or exposing crime or serious impropriety.

ii) Protecting public health and safety.

iii) Preventing the public from being misled by an action or statement of an individual or organisation.

2. There is a public interest in freedom of expression itself.

3. Whenever the public interest is invoked, the PCC will require editors to demonstrate fully how the public interest was served.

4. The PCC will consider the extent to which material is already in the public domain, or will become so.

5. In cases involving children under 16, editors must demonstrate an exceptional public interest to override the normally paramount interest of the child.

(Source: PCC website: www.pcc.org.uk)

One complainant said that the *Dorset Echo* had revealed his cystic fibrosis in a piece entitled 'Mum's Plea over Organ Donations'. Although his mother had spoken to the newspaper, the PCC concluded the man had not given permission for his photograph or details to be published. In the second case, the *Wiltshire Gazette and Herald* apologised for the fact that they had published a photograph of an elderly woman in a car accident before all her family knew of the situation. In the third, *OK!* magazine printed a picture of a male celebrity and the complainant outside an Alcoholics Anonymous meeting, thus revealing her treatment. The complaint was upheld.

Revealing health records in the public interest was also an argument in a recent case heard at the European Court of Human Rights in Strasbourg (*Case of Biriuk v Lithuania*[47]). The applicant, a 38-year-old woman, complained after her HIV-positive status was revealed in a front-page story of Lithuania's biggest newspaper. She won her original case in the Vilnius Third District Court (which found the paper had published the details in order to boost sales): but when she took her case to the Supreme Court claiming more compensation, it dismissed the appeal, saying *inter alia* that people who lived in proximity to the applicant had been concerned about their safety which was 'endangered by [her] behaviour which does not always meet moral standards'. (See para. 10 of the judgment.)

The court in Strasbourg disagreed and awarded her 6,500 euros in compensation, saying that the publication of this information could not be 'deemed to contribute to any debate of general interest to society' but rather had been done 'to satisfy the prurient curiosity of a particular readership and to boost the defendant's commercial interests' (para. 42 of the judgment). The legal arguments to and fro reveal the fine lines which exist between disclosure in the public interest, and the protection of privacy.

Are there times when revealing someone's medical history is justifiable? Once again, the investigator Nick Davies justifies the means— at least in some cases—by the ends. He tells the story of being passed, and using, the medical records of prisoners to show how the Prison Service was failing those with mental health problems:

> *The answer is always in the detail. I did a lot of stuff about mentally disordered people in prisons and got hold of their medical records. Is that over the privacy line? Yes it is ... Is it*

---

[47] 47 *Biriuk v Lithuania*, Application No. 23373/03 Judgment in Strasbourg, 25 Nov. 2008: www.menschenrechte.ac.at/orig/08_6/Biriuk.pdf

justified? Yes it is ... 70 per cent of those in prisons have two or more diagnosable conditions and the prisons just can't cope. But it isn't necessary to identify the exact prisoner.[48]

It must be recognised that here, too, celebrities can use their health problems as a means of attracting attention, and even payment. The most vivid example came in early 2009, when the *Big Brother* contestant Jade Goody, diagnosed with terminal cervical cancer, entered into a series of agreements which were reported to have brought her some £1m— including a reported £700,000 from *OK!* magazine for the exclusive rights to cover her wedding to Jack Tweed in February and christening of her sons just before she died.

Active politicians have remained, in the main, reticent. Neither Labour's Mo Mowlam, who revealed her brain tumour, nor the Liberal Democrats' Sir Menzies Campbell, who had non-Hodgkin lymphoma, were in power when their health problems came to light.

David Owen's recent book, *In Sickness and in Power,* chronicles how prime ministers and foreign leaders from Theodore Roosevelt onwards have customarily concealed details about their failing health, whether physical or mental—sometimes lying to the press to do so. Owen, who wants independent health assessments before any leader takes power, questions whether privacy in these cases serves the nation best—and appears to be arguing for less privacy in these cases:

Such illness raises many important issues: the impact on decision-making; the dangers inherent in the illness being kept secret; the difficulty of removing ill leaders, in democracies as well as in dictatorships; and not least, the responsibility that illness in heads of government places on their doctors. Should their loyalty be exclusively to their patient as would normally be the case or do they have an obligation to take into account the political health of their country?[49]

Iain Dale, the blogger, also claims that, far from journalists invading privacy, more is concealed over health than revealed:

---

[48] Interview, Lewes, 6 Aug. 2008.
[49] D. Owen, *In Sickness and in Power: Illness in Heads of Government over the Past 100 Years* (Methuen, 2008).

I think if a politician lied about any aspect of their life then it is in the public interest to reveal that. Charles Kennedy [the former Lib Dem leader] had said he didn't have a drink problem. Yet Paxo [Jeremy Paxman, presenter of BBC2's Newsnight] got slated when he raised it. I've always been uncomfortable with the lobby system—journos keep secrets in return for access. That's distinctly unhealthy.[50]

A recent story in the *Evening Standard* claimed the Duke of Edinburgh had prostate cancer. The Palace took the odd step of complaining to the Press Complaints Commission under both articles 1 and 3 of the code:[51] saying the story was not only inaccurate but also that it breached the Duke's privacy. The *Standard* later published an apology,[52] the first time according to the *Daily Telegraph* that a member of the Royal Family has had a complaint over privacy upheld by the PCC. 'This is a highly significant ruling,' one royal source told the *Telegraph's* columnist Andrew Pierce. 'It establishes that members of the Royal family are entitled to privacy too.'[53]

Finally, one change in health reporting is that the PCC has taken a much firmer line recently about revealing someone's pregnancy in the first twelve weeks. After complaints by the actress Joanna Riding (upheld against the *Independent*) and the singer Charlotte Church (upheld against *The Sun*) the Commission stated clearly: 'newspapers should not reveal the fact of someone's pregnancy before the 12 week scan without consent'.[54]

Family life

Relatives have frequently been the first port of call for any reporter involved in a story—whether it's the wife of a murder victim (or murderer) or the grown-up child of someone who has suddenly become famous. In crime stories, relatives are routinely approached to 'stand up' the story, and give valuable detail; one of a rookie reporter's first jobs is inevitably the

[50] Interview, London, 9 Sept. 2008.
[51] O. Luft, 'Palace Complains to PCC over Philip Cancer Story', 7 Aug. 2008:
www.guardian.co.uk/media/2008/aug/07/royalsandthemedia.privacy
[52] www.thisislondon.co.uk/standard/article-23529084-details/HRH+The+Duke+of+Edinburgh:+Apology/article.do
[53] A. Pierce, 'Prince Philip Given Front Page Apology over Cancer Report', *Daily Telegraph*, 8 Aug. 2008: www.telegraph.co.uk/global/main.jhtml?xml=/global/2008/08/08/noindex/royal.xml
[54] PCC ruling, *Charlotte Church v the Sun*, 3 May 2007. www.pcc.org.uk/cases/adjudicated.html?article=NDUzMA==

'doorstep' (trying to get the subject of a story or a relative to comment) or the death knock (asking a family to comment after someone's death).

While such reporting can be intrusive and gratuitous, it can ensure that the family's view is reported and it can avoid inaccurate speculation. The reality is that some people do want to give 'their side of the story', as the old newspaper justification terms it.

The problems usually arise around those who are targeted merely because they are related to someone famous. Siblings of the royal girlfriends, Kate Middleton and Chelsy Davy, have found embarrassing pictures of themselves turning up in the tabloids: James Middleton in drag, Shaun Davy sharing a pair of shorts with his sister.

In many cases where there is a genuine story to be unearthed, an unofficial 'deal' is done. Former Deputy Prime Minister John Prescott managed to keep details of his wife's secret child (born when she was a teenager) out of the papers for three years under article 3 of the PCC code—but eventually cooperated with *The Sun* when Pauline Prescott and her son wanted to be seen in public together.[55] Some years earlier former minister Clare Short, who was reunited with the son she had given up for adoption at the age of 18, chose to give the story to Suzanne Moore of the *Independent* in the hopes of controlling the situation.[56]

Private conversations

A further challenge to journalists is whether overheard conversations, clearly or apparently private, should remain so, and in what circumstances. At the 2008 Labour Party conference, two stories—both later denied— revolved around private conversations apparently 'overheard' by journalists. David Miliband comparing his speech to a 'Heseltine moment' was heard by a BBC journalist in a lift;[57] and Ruth Kelly allegedly calling Gordon Brown's speech 'terrible' was linked by Conservatives to an *Observer* journalist, Toby Helm (Helm denied hearing any such thing[58]). In November 2008 the *Sunday Mirror* journalist Adam Lee-Potter found himself a row in front of the Liberal Democrat leader Nick Clegg on a flight from Gatwick to Inverness, in which Clegg allegedly spent the time denigrating members of his shadow cabinet to policy advisers (various Lib

---

[55] K. Ahmed, 'Prescott "Joy" at Family Reunion', *Guardian*, 3 Aug. 2003: www.guardian.co.uk/politics/2003/aug/03/uk.politicalnews

[56] S. Moore, 'Clare's Baby—and Her Happy Ending', *Independent*, 17 Oct 1996.

[57] BBC website, 'Miliband "Heseltine" Moment Fear', 23 Sept. 2008: http://news.bbc.co.uk/1/hi/uk_politics/7630532.stm

[58] T. Helm, 'The "Awful" Truth about Ruth Kelly and Gordon Brown', *Guardian* blogs, 24 Sept. 2008: www.guardian.co.uk/politics/blog/2008/sep/24/labourconference.ruthkelly

Dems were denigrated as 'useless', '[not] emotionally intelligent' and 'a pain in the a***'[59]).

The varying and entertaining accounts of who said what to whom in or off a yacht in Corfu in the summer of 2008—involving politicians, financiers and Russian billionaires—are the bread-and-butter of political reporting. If these words were said in public, then journalists have the right to report them. But if they had been said in private? Nathaniel Rothschild, the financier at the centre of the Corfu reporting, evidently thought that it was all private, as his subsequent correspondence to *The Times* shows[60]— but is there a difference between reporting private conversations about how two government ministers get on and those concerning allegations over donations sought? As Mr Justice Eady has suggested: 'Public office implies public scrutiny but there is a line around private, inchoate conversations. People must be allowed to think aloud.'[61]

Finance

This is seen as much more straightforward, especially where public finance is involved. A former Insight reporter for *The Sunday Times* told us: 'I was never stopped from doing a story because of privacy. I don't think it's as much of a problem in business stories. Whenever we were doing political or sport stories it was usually about money—public money.'[62] That journalist claimed that most of their information came from careful investigation of what was already in the public domain, using the Freedom of Information Act, or what could be found by going to Companies' House or looking in the register of interests: '99.9 per cent of our information is obtained through conversations with people who have often got an axe to grind—and often have the documents to prove the story themselves—so data protection is not so much of an issue.'[63]

David Leigh agrees: he defines much of 'public interest' to be concerned with money: 'impropriety, bribery, crimes … misdemeanours, waste of public money' and that he did not find that issues of privacy came up in that respect. Where he found a problem was with the use of private investigators (of which, more later) who would trawl through financial

---

[59] A. Lee-Potter, 'Exclusive: Liberal Democrat Leader Nick Clegg Slags Off His Own Party Colleagues on a Packed Plane', *Sunday Mirror*, 29 Nov. 2008: www.mirror.co.uk/news/top-stories/2008/11/29/lib-dumb-liberal-democrat-leader-nick-clegg-slags-off-his-own-party-colleagues-on-packed-plane-115875-20934579

[60] N. Rothschild, Letter to the Editor, *The Times*, 21 Oct. 2008: www.timesonline.co.uk/tol/news/politics/article4982254.ece

[61] Interview, London, 17 Jan. 2008.

[62] Phone interview, 3 Sept. 2008.

[63] Phone interview, 3 Sept. 2008.

records for journalists in the hope of turning up something juicy:

> *It's completely wrong to break the law to get private detectives to get phone information, credit card information as a first resort just to get dirty details about people which might or not make a story.*[64]

Where do we have the right to be private?

'When I started doing *heat* in 1999, privacy and what we understood by it was what went on inside people's homes and behind closed doors,' says Mark Frith.

> *We wouldn't take pictures through someone's windows or on private property—and that was what we understood by privacy—a not very sophisticated understanding. This has changed and there is now a different idea of privacy—but I would say there is some confusion at the moment, the problem is we don't know where we stand.*[65]

But the home, according to Chris Wessun of ITV, is not part of this confusion: it remains 'inviolable'.[66] A recent example is a PCC ruling against footage that the *Scarborough Evening News* put on its website, following a police raid. Officers were seen examining the personal belongings and bedroom of the absent householder, against whom no charges were ever brought.[67] Kevin Marsh of the BBC College of Journalism is equally clear: 'Even if there was an overriding public interest, we would take a hard line on avoiding the use of anything filmed from a public space into a private space.'[68]

This however does not stretch to the banning of the 'doorstep' and the gathering of journalists outside the home of someone in the public arena. But issues do arise if the journalistic pack refuses to accept that there will be 'no comment' or no picture and does not disperse. The PCC has been known to approach editors to call them off. Indeed whole communities,

[64] Interview, London, 4 Nov. 2008.
[65] Phone interview, 10 Sept. 2008.
[66] Interview, London, 14 July 2008.
[67] *Carolyn Popple and Scarborough Evening News* -
www.pcc.org.uk/cases/adjudicated.html?article=NTE0OQ==
[68] Interview, London, 13 Aug. 2008.

such as Dunblane and Soham, have made such requests in the aftermath of tragedy.

Hospitals, too, are now seen as no-go areas. The Kaye case as mentioned earlier was seen as a nadir. In its aftermath, judges started to rework the law of confidence to find some redress—not just for those in hospitals but the concept of a 'private life'. The arrival of the Human Rights Act in 2000 strengthened their hand. (This will be discussed more fully later.) Certainly there would now be little support for any journalist trying to do something similar to what the *Sport* did to Kaye. The test will always be as set out by Mr Justice Eady:

> *Is there a reasonable expectation of privacy, if not that is the end of the matter … Has there been misbehaviour even within the home, e.g. tax evasion, domestic abuse, or what amounts to criminal or antisocial behaviour, that would eliminate a reasonable expectation? What would the judgement of a reasonable person be: what would they expect to know?*[69]

Of course, it begs the questions: who is that reasonable person and what is a reasonable expectation? Added to that (again discussed later), celebrities such as Naomi Campbell and J. K. Rowling have attempted to argue that they and their families should have protection from invasions of privacy when walking along a public street.

Conclusion

The judgments become ever more challenging: but the trends are now becoming clearer. On the one hand, those in the public gaze do, when they can, seek to leverage selected parts of their private life through a complaisant media by mutually advantageous deals, while protecting other parts they don't wish to expose through the courts. Those public figures who cannot, in the main, make such deals—classically, politicians—are also seeking to protect their private lives against media which are generally sceptical of their justification for doing so. The courts—usually, but not exclusively, in the person of Mr Justice Eady, the leading media judge, who, through his judgments has made himself into something of a hate figure in the eyes of tabloid editors—now take a more critical view of intrusion into private life than they did, including the private life of celebrities.

[69] Interview, London, 17 Jan. 2008.

2. New technology, new challenges to privacy

The old media have wrestled with the dilemmas we have discussed in Chapter 1 for many years. New technology, allied to a changing public mood, brings a new dimension. The arrival of the internet and the growth of digital technology have produced new privacy challenges—one of the largest of which is the fact that people are giving away private information about themselves both wittingly and unwittingly, without realising how it might be used.

A new mood is at work, which regards the web as a playroom where you can create both fact and fiction around your persona—and find as many friends as possible to share it with. Invention, exaggeration and pure lies seem unremarkable, while photos you might think twice about sharing in real life are posted up, seemingly without a blush.

Yet at the same time, a YouGov survey shows that privacy is valued above freedom of speech and open access—even among 18–24 year olds.[70] And while the real world has been protected by the law of defamation that prevents many rumours (and truths) from appearing in the mainstream media, we are still struggling to cope with the relatively unregulated virtual world of the internet and blogging.

However, that seems to be changing. Last year, Mathew Firsht, a businessman whose personal details were 'laid bare' in fake entries on the Facebook website, succeeded in a libel action. He was awarded £22,000 in damages against an old school friend, who created a false personal profile of him and a company profile called 'Has Mathew Firsht lied to you?' Private information concerning his whereabouts, activities and

---

[70] Edwards and Fieschi, *UK Confidential*, 62.

relationship status as well as false statements about his sexual orientation and political views formed part of the fake profile.[71]

The mainstream media have greedily feasted on the virtual world as a new source for information about individuals and stories. 'We used to look on *Friends Reunited*—how long ago and primitive that seems,' mused the former Insight reporter.[72] Many journalists are taking advantage of the wealth of private information that is being exposed via the internet—particularly on social networking sites such as Facebook, MySpace and shared sites like YouTube—to find material for their own stories, with little discussion of the ethics of doing so. The result is that this information is often used in ways never foreseen by those who originally put it there.

You may not immediately recognise the name Amanda Knox (at the time of writing, on trial for the murder of Meredith Kercher, a British exchange student who died in November 2007 in Perugia). You are more likely to have heard of 'FoxyKnoxy'—the name Knox gave herself on her MySpace page, where (helpfully for journalists) she had also posted short stories that involved a drugging and rape scenario of a young girl, and a picture of herself posing with a gun. A YouTube video of her drunk at university[73] also emerged, while Knox's boyfriend Raffaelo Sollecito's blog pictured him with a machete. This was all used in articles such as the *Daily Mail's* exposé of 7 November 2007: 'FoxyKnoxy: Inside the Twisted World of Flatmate Suspected of Meredith's Murder'.[74] Invasion of privacy? The truth was, the vast majority of the information had been put into the public domain by Ms Knox herself.

The attitude of most mainstream media journalists to their use of Facebook, MySpace and YouTube to collect information is thus essentially that private citizens willingly put this information into the public domain, therefore it is fine to use it. As Tom Crone puts it:

> *The internet makes it easier to do investigations now—the information is out there on Facebook, MySpace and half the time they don't hit the privacy button ... I think if you ... don't hit the privacy button ... you have a real problem suggesting that what you have put up there is private.*[75]

[71] Firsht judgment can be found at www.onebrickcourt.com/cases_files/119firsht.pdf

[72] Phone interview, 3 Sept. 2008.

[73] 'YouTube Video of FoxyKnoxy Drunk While at University', *Daily Mail*, 2 Nov. 2007. The piece is un-bylined and the video has now been removed from YouTube's site. www.dailymail.co.uk/news/article-492300/YouTube-video-FoxyKnoxy-drunk-university.html

[74] C. Fernandez and B. Hale, 'FoxyKnoxy: Inside the Twisted World of Flatmate Suspected of Meredith's Murder', *Daily Mail*, 7 Nov. 2007: www.dailymail.co.uk/news/article-492092/Foxy-Knoxy-Inside-twisted-world-flatmate-suspected-Merediths-murder.html

[75] Interview, London, 10 Sept. 2008.

David Leigh of the *Guardian* was equally scathing of those who posted information or pictures on sites like Facebook and then tried to cry abuse of privacy afterwards:

> *Yes of course they [journalists] are justified in using it. If you want to put stuff about yourself up in the public domain … and people can make what use of it they like. I don't see any point in complaining about it. If you don't want the information out there, don't put it out there … I think the interesting question revolves round copyright—if you put a picture up, are you authorising people to copy your picture? You give away the information, but do you give away the right to reproduce the picture? If you put a picture of yourself drunk or sober on Facebook and some broadcaster wants to purloin it, that's because it's got a commercial value to them and you should have the rights over whether willing to sell it or not. So it's not about privacy but about who has rights over the material.*[76]

Yet most people using the playpen of a social networking site do regard it at the very least as semi-private. They are likely to draw a distinction in their own minds between sharing a photo with online 'friends' and seeing it reproduced in *The Sun*. Rachel North, the blogger who survived the bombings in London on 7 July 2005, says that when she started to blog about her experience, she chose to conceal some information about herself—such as her real name and certain details about her experience of the bombing. She believes that many people are not taking their privacy seriously.

> *The thing about the Facebook generation, if you grow up with CCTV everywhere, pictures on Facebook, emails and BlackBerries everywhere, camera phones, I wonder whether young people are growing up with a different idea of what privacy is. You see things like Big Brother where people are flaying themselves on TV … I don't know if those people have a concept of privacy.*[77]

Zoe Margolis, the sex-life blogger, had thought that being anonymous meant no one would ever try to discover her true identity. She had not told anyone about her double life—even when she received a book deal for her explicit writing.

[76] Interview, London, 4 Nov. 2008.
[77] Interview, London, 28 July 2008.

In retrospect, I probably left too many clues. But I did try to hide myself. I said which industry I worked in but not which department. I didn't talk about my family or friends in detail and I combined characteristics. I only used initials. I didn't describe my body in any detail. I had anonymity so I was truthful—about my emotions, the sex I had—much to my embarrassment now. I thought I was writing for blokes—so that they might put down the crap porn and think and try to relate the women they were with much better.[78]

Margolis was unmasked following the media frenzy over explicit blogs sparked by the success of the blogger Belle de Jour. That 'blog' claimed to be the anonymous account of a London callgirl. The media tried—and failed—to discover the identity of Belle and whether her story was true: in the aftermath, other sexually explicit blogs became part of the news agenda including Margolis's.

However, she who is humiliated by the net can also use the net to humiliate. The *Sunday Times* had tried and failed to get Margolis to respond to their story, despite promising a photo shoot (the suggestion was that she bring along some 'colourful evening wear' to pose in) and the chance to (in that classic newspaper phrase) put her side of the story. In a familiar ploy (see the Mosley case), Margolis says that Nicholas Hellen, the then news editor, said if she did not cooperate he would publish details about her mother. She decided to turn Hellen's threat back on him.

I showed [Hellen's emails] to my mum and said I don't want you dragged into it. I didn't want it to affect her business—which it did. But Mum said 'f*** them don't even dignify that with a response' … So I didn't. They never got anything from me. Five months later on the anniversary of the blog I printed that [Hellen's email] and people were livid and started a googlebomb. That means thousands linked that blog page on their blog highlighting Nicholas Hellen. And so if you googled Nicholas Hellen it would come up Nicholas Hellen is a **** or look what NH did to Abby Lee [Margolis's alter ego on the blog]. It's a way of getting back at newspapers that celebrities don't have.[79]

---

[78] Interview, London, 7 Aug. 2008.
[79] Interview, London, 7 Aug. 2008.

Kevin Marsh of the BBC believes the mainstream media have made up the rules for this area as they went along:

> *I don't think we've even begun to work out the limits of social networking sites. There's no doubt most teenagers don't think when they post to Facebook they don't think it is public ... they see it as a public private space. It's like a conversation in the pub— it's in a public space, but not everyone and their uncle can eavesdrop. I don't know where the limits lie—when you have a student killed on a gap year is it legit to use photos of the gap year? Probably. Is it legit to use postings intended for a couple of people to read? I don't know.*[80]

Roger Mahony of the BBC's Editorial Policy team pointed out that if the BBC used such a picture it would make it available to a much wider public than a personal website that could only be found with very specific search criteria. There is a responsibility 'to consider the impact of its reuse on the grieving and distressed'.[81]

Roger Mahony of the BBC has developed some rules for working with information culled from social sites, which include:

- You shouldn't assume pictures are what they purport to be—verify.
- The ease of availability of pictures does not remove the responsibility to consider their sensitivity.
- Consider degrees of public domain. The use of a picture by the BBC or other media brings material to a much wider public than a personal website that would only be found with very specific search criteria. (Does the fact that material has been put into the public domain give the media the right to exploit its existence without regard to the consequences?)
- The publication of a picture on a personal website does not mean the owner intended it to be available for all purposes and circumstances.
- There is a responsibility to consider the intrusion into grief and the impact of its reuse on the grieving and distressed.
- There are also issues of privacy and copyright. Fair dealing doesn't extend to photographs and there are risks of infringement of privacy and copyright if there is no strong public interest for using a photo.

Camilla Wright of Popbitch believes there is a change in attitude between younger and older generations such that, even when today's teenagers grow up to become more sober thirty and fortysomethings, the idea of putting phone pictures online or other information will have become the

---

[80] Interview, London, 13 Aug. 2008.
[81] Interview, London, 19 Aug. 2008.

norm. 'I can't imagine people will stop doing it because it's normalised now—in the same way as my dad never put TV on as a matter of course at home, while I would not think of not automatically switching it on.'[82] She said a lawyer had told her of interviewing young people for jobs—to find that, on their Facebook pages later that day, they had instigated discussions about the interview, and whether the job would be worth having. Areas previously thought of as sacred were, she said, now up for grabs online:

> *I even heard yesterday that a local newspaper was doing a Twitter feed from a funeral—'the coffin is going up aisle, the grieving widow is behind it' etc. etc.—even those things you think you would take a step back from. Illness death birth—all these are not necessarily private.*[83]

Kevin Marsh was also aware that journalists were abusing social networking sites for research purposes:

> *Bilawal Bhutto is at college with my son. When Bilawal's mother [Benazir] was murdered there were hundreds of false Facebook and My Space sites 'set up by Bilawal' to try to get information or photographs. They were set up by journalists saying things like 'I've lost all my photos of my mates, can you repost them'. I can't think of the real life equivalent of that. It's like breaking into someone's house and stealing their photo album.*[84]

Google—the real threat to privacy?

Google has had among the most profound effects of all the new technologies. It has come to dominate the world of search engines—through the data it collects on users' searches, through new applications such as Street View and by allowing people to find information which previously might have been left to moulder away in newspaper libraries. This fame has meant that it has had to defend itself against accusations that it has the power to make people's lives less private. When Street View—a map service involving thousands of street-level pictures—was launched in 2007, it immediately faced criticism for possible privacy

---

[82] Interview, London, 7 Oct. 2008.
[83] Interview, London, 7 Oct. 2008.
[84] Interview, London, 13 Aug. 2008.

implications, since people were identifiable from the pictures.[85] As Google rolled out the product in the UK, there were more complaints, including a incident when the residents of Broughton in Milton Keynes refused the Street View car access to the village. As John Lanchester wrote in the *London Review of Books*:

> *It might be entertaining to look at the now-ubiquitous photo of the man coming out of the strip club, and you might argue that he deserves whatever he gets; but it's not necessarily without consequences for him, whoever he might be. As for the woman who had moved to a secret address to escape a violent partner, but was clearly identifiable on Street View, let's hope her complaint was acted on in time.[86]*

Yet as Lanchester acknowledges, people's addresses are already available via the electoral register; Street View is merely adding pictures. Perhaps this is why, despite complaints made to the privacy watchdog, in April 2009 the Information Commissioner ruled that while there was a small risk of privacy invasion, it should not be stopped.[87]

In its 2007 report, the group Privacy International also labelled Google 'hostile to privacy'.[88] It had earlier said its concerns were because of privacy implications of having a centrally located, warehouse of millions of users' searches, and that under existing US law, Google could be forced to hand over all such information to the US Government. However in early 2005, the Department of Justice attempted to force Google to comply with a subpoena for 'the text of each search string entered onto Google's search engine over a one-week period (absent any information identifying the person who entered such query)'. Peter Barron, head of communications for Google in the UK, Benelux and Ireland says:

> *We have a history of being a strong advocate for user privacy. For example in 2006, we went to court in the US to resist a Department of Justice subpoena for millions of search queries on the grounds that it was excessive and invaded our users' privacy.*

[85] S. Knight, 'All-Seeing Google Street View Provokes Privacy Fears', *The Times*, 1 June 2007: http://technology.timesonline.co.uk/tol/news/tech_and_web/article1870995.ece
[86] J. Lanchester, 'Short Cuts', *London Review of Books,* 9 Apr. 2009: www.lrb.co.uk/v31/n07/lanc01_.html
[87] 'All Clear for Google Street View', BBC News, 24 Apr. 2009: http://news.bbc.co.uk/1/hi/technology/8014178.stm
[88] www.privacyinternational.org/issues/internet/interimrankings.pdf

The judge ultimately ruled in Google's favour, establishing an important precedent for user privacy.[89]

Barron claims that 'Google puts privacy at the heart of its products' and that it has constantly evolved to address concerns; it recently announced that it would anonymise IP addresses on server logs after nine months, down from eighteen months. But he adds that individuals need to take responsibility for their actions rather than putting the full weight on search engines and internet companies, who facilitate easier transfer of information.

As individuals and users, the question is one of personal choice and judgement. Would you be happy if a future employer saw a particular photo of you at that party? You wouldn't just share personal details with someone you met in the street, so is it really wise to give them to someone you just met online.[90]

He also champions the ability of search engines to make information much more accessible—rather than previously where it had to be sought out via books or newspaper libraries:

The internet has broken down many of the barriers that traditionally existed between people and information, and search has made it possible for people to more easily find what it is they are looking for—in effect democratising access to information. Information previously stored in books and newspapers already exists in the public domain. But having content like this online prevents it becoming lost and inaccessible.[91]

The invulnerability of the new media?

While the laws of libel, as we have seen in the Firsht case, do apply, bloggers rarely run the risk of being taken to court, since the perceived rewards would be so small. Says Iain Dale: 'Though bloggers are subject to the same libel law as anyone else there is a feeling that you can get away

---

[89] Interview, London, 14 Oct. 2008.
[90] Interview, London, 14 Oct. 2008.
[91] Interview, London, 14 Oct. 2008.

with more on the basis that no one is likely to sue you because you haven't got any money. Some bloggers take that to an extreme …'[92] Dale feels that bloggers have pushed the boundaries very far—'they publish items no gossip columns would ever do'—and cited the example of an item by political blogger Guido Fawkes where Fawkes, in dealing with the story of Ivan Lewis, a Labour minister who had allegedly been harassing a former member of staff via text, described him as 'not safe in taxis' along with another Conservative MP, also named. '[That MP] is now faced with dilemma that it's now on the internet insinuating that though he's married he goes after women.'

Dale says he has now retreated from this sort of political gossip, but does admit the part he played in breaking details about the Tracy Temple–John Prescott affair which had not previously made it into the public domain. He confesses to a split view: on the one hand, he acknowledges the net's excesses: on the other, he feels them to be justified because of the familiar charge of hypocrisy.

> *The Mail on Sunday had serialized Tracy Temple's diaries. I was then offered extracts they hadn't printed; about Viagra and size of his manhood. I wrote a fairly innocuous piece and put extracts on my blog. The Sun rang me and the next day the whole of page 7 was '2 inch size of Prezza's manhood revealed'. The traffic on the blog that day went mad. Then there were rumours about an affair Prescott had also had with a Labour minister and Guido kept dropping hints and so did I but none of the newspapers would touch it. Guido even named her. … [I]f it had been a Tory minister [the journalists] would have done it but they were not willing to dish it out to Prezza and I think that's hypocritical.*[93]

In fact mainstream media, while resentful of the net's freedom, will on occasion use it as a 'laundry' for dirty stories. Camilla Wright says that she has been approached by mainstream media eager to know whether Popbitch would run this or that contentious story. In one particular case, involving the family of a public figure, she was approached by the BBC and others: 'People at the BBC were saying if Popbitch does it, we will. I've had this with a few cases … "if you do it—we can follow" … but I don't want to be a test case—and in this case I think we were right [not to run the story].'[94]

[92] Interview, London, 9 Sept. 2008.
[93] Interview, London, 9 Sept. 2008.
[94] Interview, London, 7 Oct. 2008.

Many are increasingly concerned about the rumour mill on the web going beyond embarrassingly sexual detail. On 15 September 2008, Sir Tim Berners-Lee the originator of the World Wide Web called for an end to the 'thinking of cults', by which he meant the malicious and damaging rumours spread via the internet, and he has set up the World Wide Web Foundation to offer kite marks to websites it deems to have reputable information.[95]

As this report was going to press, another scandal erupted within the British government thanks to Paul Staines/Guido Fawkes. Damian McBride, an aide to Prime Minister Gordon Brown, was discovered by Staines to have been plotting with two other former/present Labour aides, Derek Draper and Charlie Whelan, to put into circulation on the web a series of rumours about leading opposition figures and, in one case, a wife (of shadow Chancellor George Osborne). This was planned to be the star content on a new website, RedRag.

The ensuing scandal saw McBride resign and the Prime Minister write letters of 'regret' for his aide's actions to those targeted[96] and, after a delay of some days, he apologised. The event, an ugly one, appeared, however, to show that the conduct of politics today now demands the kind of character assassination skills which McBride displayed in his series of emails.

Once political parties and programmes decline in importance, once the news media become increasingly concerned with the reporting of personality and once the internet—with its instant response ability, its tendency to destroy secrets and its vast memory—becomes the dominant medium, then scandal, gossip and personality come into the foreground as major elements in the political struggle.

The coverage of politics on the web focuses as much on the personal as the political. Dale and Staines believe that conventional political coverage in the UK is the preserve of a cosy journalist/politician elite, in which secrets are kept rather than revealed, and scandals routinely covered up. The 'personal is political' was a radical feminist cry of the 1960s, meaning that such issues as abortion, contraception and sexual orientation were fit subjects for campaigns and legislative action. It is now pressed into service as a catch-all rationale for reporting which invades space which men and women in public life had wished, for good reasons and bad, to keep private.

---

[95] P. Ghosh, 'Warning Sounded on Web's Future', BBC News, 15 Sept. 2008:
www.news.bbc.co.uk/1/hi/technology/7613201.htm
[96] P. Webster, 'Gordon Brown Apologises for Damian McBride Email Smears Scandal', *The Times,* 16 Apr. 2009: http://www.timesonline.co.uk/tol/news/politics/article6105105.ece

The would-be reputation assassins all believe that the personal is where political battles should be fought. In the case of McBride and Whelan, it has been their practice. In the case of Draper—who took time off fulltime political work to train as a psychotherapist—he has articulated, in lectures and in articles, a view that the characters of public men and women should be a subject of examination, analysis and revelation. This is both because these interest the public more, and because, at a time when there are no deep differences in policies, the character of leaders is more important than their programmes.

It may be possible to do what the Prime Minister said he wished to do: present an administration to which destructive tactics and spin would be foreign. There are, to be sure, significant lines to be drawn—which the Prime Minister is trying, once more, to convince the country that he can draw—between glitz and debasement. But the net's intrinsic characteristics, coupled with the trends in both the media and in politics, make that an extraordinarily hard aspiration to achieve.

One last thing worth noting in this story is about the interaction of the net and mainstream media. The fact that McBride suggested using a blog to spread false rumours demonstrated how the internet is seen as a way of sidestepping the more cautious attitude taken by the mainstream media. However Staines did not in the end publish the emails himself, despite taunting McBride and Draper on his website; he gave the emails to the *News of the World* and the *Sunday Times*, who brought the story to more general attention.

Conclusion

The net has opened a parallel universe to that of the mainstream media—one with which everyone is learning to cope. In this vast universe, facts and rumours, lies and truth, facts and conspiracy theories, jostle for attention and for primacy, as Berners-Lee fears. On the current evidence, it has given those who use it the ability for the most part to act in a less constrained way than those working under the laws, regulations and traditions of the mainstream media when it comes to intrusion and invasion of privacy. The lifting of these inhibitions gives the net the attractive prospect of freedom: it also allows it to trespass much more efficiently and with much greater impunity into areas where others are more reluctant to tread.

3. Privacy and the longer arm of the law

We have noted that the law is now changing its practice in the face of a growing number of cases taken to preserve privacy—and, perhaps, a growing number of intrusions of privacy. Here, we want to examine more closely how it is changing, and why.

'Privacy is the new libel', says Adam Cannon, a lawyer at the *Daily Mail*.[97] Many within the news media now believe that, even before the Mosley case, celebrities and others were increasingly using privacy, rather than defamation actions, to keep stories out of the public domain. Tom Crone at News International felt that where once cases brought were 50–50 libel–privacy, now, marginally, privacy is cited in the majority of actions taken. The Mosley trial was the defining instance of this trend to date: and the one which has brought most clearly the issues of private life and public interest into the public domain.

Why should privacy matter so much that people want to see it enshrined in law? The reason it matters is to do with the integrity of a personality (how much private space we need to grow, develop and discover who we are); and what are the legitimate expectations we have around our private life.

The shift—from an assumption of the right to privacy to the perceived need to protect it—proceeded above all from the devastating human consequences in the last century of both fascism and communism, and the state-backed power of the secret police over private lives, and even thoughts. These then produced a need for legislation and international treaties which protected the individual, most of all, from the state.

At the end of the Second World War, the Universal Declaration of Human Rights was one of the first acts of the new United Nations. Article

---

[97] Interview, London, 10 Sept. 2008.

12 reads: 'No one shall be subjected to arbitrary interference with his privacy, family, home or correspondence, nor to attacks upon his honour and reputation. Everyone has the right to the protection of the law against such interference or attacks.' It was followed in Europe by the European Convention on Human Rights—drafted by British lawyers—for the benefit of those who had felt the harsh and intrusive hand of totalitarian government (see box).

It, in turn, was eventually incorporated into British law with the Human Rights Act (HRA) of 1998—an incorporation which remains contested by some politicians and by sections of the press, who (see below) see it as a curb to press freedom and investigative reporting. But the Convention is also carefully drafted to balance potentially competing rights, for example, the right to privacy, with that of freedom of expression. There is also recognition of other competing claims such as national security.

Article 8
1. Everyone has the right to respect for his private and family life, his home and his correspondence.
2. There shall be no interference by a public authority with the exercise of this right except such as is in accordance with the law and is necessary in a democratic society in the interests of national security, public safety or the economic well-being of the country, for the prevention of disorder or crime, for the protection of health or morals, or for the protection of the rights and freedoms of others.

Article 10
1. Everyone has the right to freedom of expression. This right shall include freedom to hold opinions and to receive and impart information and ideas without interference by public authority and regardless of frontiers. This article shall not prevent States from requiring the licensing of broadcasting, television or cinema enterprises.
2. The exercise of these freedoms, since it carries with it duties and responsibilities, may be subject to such formalities, conditions, restrictions or penalties as are prescribed by law and are necessary in a democratic society, in the interests of national security, territorial integrity or public safety, for the prevention of disorder or crime, for the protection of health or morals, for the protection of the reputation or the rights of others, for preventing the disclosure of information received in confidence, or for maintaining the authority and impartiality of the judiciary.

(Source: European Convention on Human Rights)

The interests of journalism, both commercial and professional, are served by an emphasis on Article 10—freedom of expression and freedom of the press. Sufferers at the hands of those threatening their privacy, like Rachel North and Zoe Margolis, are, unsurprisingly, in favour of a privacy law being passed, feeling—as North says—that most judges would always privilege Article 10 over Article 8. However she adds that: 'If you go back through case law, privacy does trump the right to report on people. Because people can live without knowing information on public or private figures. There's a point where a human being has to live as a functioning human being and needs a private life.'[98]

The model laid out in the HRA assumes that rights and responsibilities lie not just between the state and the individual, but between individual and corporation, and individual and individual: what has been described as a shift from the vertical to the horizontal. Where once human rights were thought to be solely about the citizen and the state (the vertical), increasingly now the courts seek to protect rights as between citizens (the horizontal). Lord Justice Sedley has described it as 'a progressive realignment of a number of human rights from the restrictions on the power of the state to positive standards of human conduct'.[99]

So in family law, the respect for family life is not simply a matter between the individual and the state but affects every dispute between parents about custody and access. It also involves the concept of proportionality, balancing any interference with a right. The bulk of individual rights are heavily qualified in the interests of the social whole.

The right to free speech, for example, is conditional on using it within proportionate legal restraints. As Oliver Wendell Holmes, the American jurist, put it in 1919, there is no such thing at the right to shout 'fire' falsely in a crowded theatre: one right cannot be used to injure the rights of another.

In Lord Sedley's view, 'we have embarked on a rebalancing of our libel law by dovetailing the Article 8 privacy right more precisely than before with the Article 10 right of free expression, each of them involving respect for others in equal measure with personal liberty'.[100] He notes the impact this has had on the development of a law of privacy, shielding people against the media.

In his judgment in the Mosley case, Mr Justice Eady put it like this:

> *In deciding whether a right has been infringed, and in assessing the relative worth of competing rights, it is not for judges to make individual moral judgments or to be swayed by personal distaste. It is not simply a matter of personal privacy versus the public*

---

[98] Interview, London, 28 July 2008.
[99] S. Sedley, 'Towards a Right to Privacy', *London Review of Books*, 5 June 2006.
[100] Ibid.

interest. The modern perception is that there is a public interest in respecting personal privacy. It is thus a question of taking account of conflicting public interest considerations and evaluating them according to increasingly well recognized criteria.[101]

The four key points in the balancing exercise were set out by Lord Steyn in a case involving a child (*In re S* [2005] 1 AC 593[102]) where an injunction was sought (and refused) to prevent the naming of a defendant in a criminal trial so that the child was not identified. The points were, first, neither value has precedence; second, where values are in conflict, judges must apply an intense focus on their comparative importance; third, they must take into account the justification for restricting a right, and, fourth, they must apply a proportionality test.

To put it more simply, as Mr Justice Eady did (in an interview for this project in January 2008 before the Mosley case), one should ask first,

Is there a reasonable expectation of privacy, if not that is the end of the matter … Then: has there been misbehaviour even within the home, e.g. tax evasion, domestic abuse, or what amounts to criminal or antisocial behaviour, that would eliminate a reasonable expectation? What would the judgement of a reasonable person be: what would they expect to know? Is there a public interest? Was it in a public or private place: where are you, who are you, what are you doing? Everything depends on the facts of the case. That is where the intense focus comes in.[103]

The testimonies of Sedley, Eady and Steyn point to more than a change in the legislation: they point, as Sedley says, to a realisation that the state in democratic societies is no longer seen to pose the actual or even potential threat it once did: but that other, non-state actors can and do. Among these, increasingly, are numbered the news media.

This makes the challenge for the journalist and the editorial process ever more testing. A number of stories and cases make the point. Over the past few years, we have had opportunity to see a three-cornered contest between those in public or semi-public life, the media in its various forms, and the courts, over where private rights begin and end, plus what the

---

[101] *Mosley v News Group* (July 2008), para. 130. The entire judgment can be found at http://news.bbc.co.uk/1/shared/bsp/hi/pdfs/24_07_08mosleyvnewsgroup.pdf
[102] For the judgment see www.publications.parliament.uk/pa/ld200304/ldjudgmt/jd041028/inres-1.htm
[103] Interview, London, 17 Jan. 2008.

public interest might be in seeing private lives exposed to a wider gaze.

A number of quite separate instances give flesh to the lawyers' arguments: and point up the way in which the law works in concrete terms.

Clive Goodman: a breach of the criminal law

In the summer of 2006, the *News of the World's* royal correspondent, Clive Goodman, was arrested and subsequently charged along with a private investigator Glenn Mulcaire with illegally intercepting mobile phone calls and text messages belonging to members of the Royal Family and other members of the royal household as well as others in public life. In 2007, he pleaded guilty to conspiracy to intercept phone messages and was sentenced to four months' imprisonment. Goodman and Mulcaire—the latter was paid more than £100,000 a year by the *News of the World*—had made more than 600 calls to royal household staff in order to extract private phone messages from voicemail. In this case, the need to balance the right of free speech—Goodman's publication of stories about the Royal Family—with privacy was not invoked. The criminal offence obviated any consideration of the rights of Goodman or the *News of the World*.

Information Commissioner: the investigators investigated

The former Commissioner Richard Thomas published two special reports in 2006 and 2007 entitled *What Price Privacy?*[104] and *What Price Privacy Now?*[105] listing publications in which he claimed up to 305 journalists had used illegal means to access personal data. This usually happened, he said, by employing third parties able to hack or bribe their way into information such as phone records that constitute private information.

The Information Commissioner sought to change the law so that conviction could attract a prison sentence of up to two years. The Government at first agreed, and then backed down in the face of pressure from newspapers. In a November 2008 speech to the Society of Editors. the editor of the *Daily Mail*, Paul Dacre, revealed why.

> *About 16 months ago, I, Les Hinton of News International and Murdoch MacLennan of the Telegraph, had dinner with Gordon Brown ... We raised a truly frightening amendment to the Data Protection Act, winding its way through parliament, under which journalists faced being jailed for two years for illicitly obtaining*

[104] See www.ico.gov.uk/upload/documents/library/corporate/research_and_reports/what_price_privacy_low_resolution.pdf
[105] See www.ico.gov.uk/upload/documents/library/corporate/research_and_reports/ico-wppnow-0602.pdf

> *personal information such as ex-directory telephone numbers or an individual's gas bills or medical records. This legislation would have made Britain the only country in the free world to jail journalists and could have had a considerable chilling effect on good journalism.*[106]

Dacre is making a strong point (though it is also, in part, factually wrong: journalists are jailed in other free countries, such as the US). He is arguing that journalists should, as a profession and irrespective of the reasons for their obtaining information, not be liable to prison sentences for doing this even if they are acting illegally.

Yet this is already a criminal offence, as the Goodman case showed: and a public interest defence is available in exceptional circumstances in support of 'responsible journalism'. (It begs the question of what 'responsible journalism' is, to which we return later.)

The Government's decision to retreat in the face of media opposition means that the status quo remains: that is, illegal information will continue to be accessed, fines will be levied and occasionally light jail sentences may be awarded when this is discovered—and media organisations will weigh up the relative worth of a scoop versus a heavy fine.

Charles Kennedy's resignation

The leader of the Liberal Democrats, Charles Kennedy, was forced to resign over his addiction to alcohol. Rumours of his lacklustre performances being fuelled by alcoholism were rife. But they had been put to Kennedy in the past—most notably by Jeremy Paxman—and firmly denied, with the support of senior party members. It was only when his inner circle lost confidence in him that the story came out—to be broken by ITN (which had just employed Kennedy's former press officer Daisy McAndrew as a political correspondent)—and Kennedy pre-empted media revelations by resigning.

Loreena McKennitt

A Canadian singer, Loreena McKennitt, successfully managed to prevent a former friend and employee from publishing details of McKennitt's private life in a book, on the grounds that there was a distinction to be drawn about what is available to anyone who happens to see the celebrity,

---

[106] Paul Dacre's speech to the Society of Editors, Bristol, 9 Nov. 2008. Full text can be found at: www.pressgazette.co.uk/story.asp?storycode=42394

and what is known by a friend or confidante who seeks to exploit that relationship of confidence. In *McKennitt v Ash* (2007) the Court of Appeal granted an injunction and awarded damages after the author had sought to write about her former friend, McKennitt, which included information about McKennitt's home, her private life and her grief following the death of her fiancé. As there was a pre-existing relationship of confidence, the questions the court asked were: is the information private in the sense that it is in principle protected by Article 8 and, if so, must the owner of the information yield to the right of freedom of expression?

Effectively, the court found that the prior relationship meant the case could be considered under breach of confidence, as it was obvious that events in a person's home cannot be 'lightly intruded upon'. Moreover, what was being told was not the reminiscences of shared experience but Ms McKennitt's own story. The court went on to reject the argument that someone who reveals or discusses information within a 'zone' of their private life has, as a result, a greatly reduced expectation of privacy in relation to other private information.

Simply because McKennitt had made limited disclosures about the death of her fiancé in a boating accident in order to raise funds for a memorial charity did not in itself open up the relationship to public scrutiny, since she was entitled to decide what private information to disclose.

One consequence of the *McKennitt* decision is to put a strain on so-called 'kiss'n'tell' stories. For example, Mr Justice Eady granted an injunction in 2006 to prevent a husband disclosing the details of an affair his wife was having with a sporting personality. His 'intense focus' was directed at the husband's vengeful conduct in seeking to sell the story and medical evidence of the potential impact on the personality's suicidal wife. Eady ruled that the cuckolded husband was entitled to exercise his freedom of expression through conversations with friends, relatives, doctors or counsellors—but not by publishing his story in the media.[107]

Not long after the McKennitt case, the Court of Appeal granted the Prince of Wales an injunction preventing the publication of his private travel journals, which had been given limited circulation to friends on a confidential basis. A newspaper had been given the journals by a former employee who had been bound by a contractual obligation of confidence. That was relevant to both the reasonable expectation of privacy and the balancing exercise.

[107] S. Webb, 'Curbs on a Modern Day Miller's Tale', *Guardian*, 11 Dec. 2006:
www.guardian.co.uk/media/2006/dec/11/mondaymediasection9

The newspaper argued that publication was in the public interest: the court replied that it was not sufficiently so as to override the confidential nature of the journal. Where a confidence had been breached the question was: 'whether in all the circumstances it is in the public interest that the duty of confidence should be breached'. On the facts, they thought not.[108]

Lord Browne

The former chief executive of BP was obliged to resign from the oil giant after he told lies in a court action in which he sought an injunction against the *Mail on Sunday* over revelations from a former lover. The former lover was seeking to make various disclosures, including alleged misuse of BP's resources, and about his relationship with Lord Browne. The courts made a careful distinction between information gained that might be in the public interest—such as actions that might have an impact on shareholders—and gossip exchanged in private dinner parties with public figures.

Mr Justice Eady and, subsequently, the Court of Appeal granted an injunction preventing the publication of allegations about the discussion of BP strategy with a third party, and remarks made in the home about work colleagues—but not about the fact of the relationship, the alleged misuse of resources or the alleged breach of confidentiality involved in discussing BP matters with the lover or showing him confidential BP documents.

This judgment is a revealing exercise in the closeness of the scrutiny the courts are now applying to the circumstances of each case. Each piece of information had to be looked at separately even though there was a previous confidential relationship between the parties. Both the nature of the information and the circumstances in which it was shared or obtained were important. They ruled there could be a reasonable expectation of confidence even in relation to trivial matters. But the Appeal Court's conclusion was that the allegations relating to Lord Browne's conduct in relation to the potential interests of BP shareholders in the use of company resources were a matter of legitimate public interest. In other words, they drew a distinction between private interactions and behaviours and those which had a potential public impact.

---

[108] J. Rozenberg, 'Prince Wins Privacy Claim over Journal', *Daily Telegraph*, 18 Mar 2006: www.telegraph.co.uk/news/uknews/1513304/Prince-wins-privacy-claim-over-journal.html

Responsible journalism

In a recent landmark judgment, the House of Lords gave encouraging support to the idea of 'responsible journalism'. It came in a defamation case involving the *Wall Street Journal* and a story about investigations into Saudi financial support for terrorism (*Jameel and others v Wall Street Journal Europe Spl*[109]). The House of Lords overthrew previous court decisions that had awarded damages to Mohammed Jameel. In his judgment on the case, Lord Hoffman quoted a Court of Appeal decision:

> *Responsible journalism is the point at which a fair balance is held between freedom of expression on matters of public concern and the reputations of individuals. Maintenance of this standard is in the public interest and in the interests of those whose reputations are involved. It can be regarded as the price journalists pay in return for the privilege … 'Responsible journalism' is a standard which everyone in the media and elsewhere can recognise. The duty–interest test based on the public's right to know, which lies at the heart of the matter, maintains the essential element of objectivity. Was there an interest or duty to publish the information and a corresponding interest or duty to receive it, having regard to its particular subject matter?*[110]

He was supported by Baroness Hale:

> *The public only have a right to be told if two conditions are fulfilled. First, there must be a real public interest in communicating and receiving the information. This is, as we all know, very different from saying that it is information which interests the public—the most vapid tittle-tattle about the activities of footballers' wives and girlfriends interests large sections of the public but no-one could claim any real public interest in our being told all about it. It is also different from the test … of whether the information is 'newsworthy'. That is too subjective a test, based on the target audience, inclinations and interests of the particular publication. There must be some real public interest in having this information in the public domain …*[111]

---

[109] The full judgment can be found at
www.publications.parliament.uk/pa/ld200506/ldjudgmt/jd061011/jamee-1.htm
[110] Ibid., para. 53
[111] Ibid., para. 47.

Jameel v WSJ was a landmark ruling which confirmed the so-called Reynolds defence—named after a case brought by the then Irish prime minister, Albert Reynolds, against the *Sunday Times* in 1994. He had objected to an article claiming he had misled parliament. After a complicated 24-day trial, Reynolds won a symbolic one penny in compensation: but the important point was the case's place in the development of British libel law. Three years later the House of Lords allowed the media to plead the 'Reynolds defence'—which meant newspapers could print untrue and defamatory information, if they could prove it was in the public interest to publish it and that it was the product of responsible journalism.

The Lords listed ten points to consider if a paper pleads qualified privilege. (One of the points was that the story must 'contain the gist' of the claimant's story. As the *Sunday Times* failed to ask Mr Reynolds for his side of the story it didn't change the case's outcome.) In *Jameel*, however, the House of Lords held that the ten criteria had been interpreted too strictly in the past. They should be seen as pointers rather than hurdles to be overcome.

Photographs: private lives and public places

A difficult area is that of photographs which are not gained by illegal means, but covertly, or via 'friends'. The *Daily Mirror* ran the photograph of Naomi Campbell to expose her 'hypocrisy' around drug abuse. The case sharpened the appetite of the courts to look at the issue of 'confidence' and whether people were misusing and publishing private and privileged information, in which there was a reasonable expectation of privacy, without consent.

In the House of Lords, there was much discussion about the fact that the photographs of Ms Campbell were taken in a public place. Could they be regarded as essentially private? There was nothing undignified about her appearance, nor was she shown in a state of distress. But the prevailing view was they were taken deliberately and in secret, and were offensive to the subject.

As Baroness Hale put it in her judgment, the fact that the photographs were taken covertly was not enough: the activity itself had to be private. A photograph of Naomi Campbell going about her daily business, such as popping to the shop for a bottle of milk, would not have infringed her privacy. In this instance, however, the connection to Narcotics

Anonymous meant her privacy was invaded. Hale's observation echoes remarks of Lord Mustill in an earlier case, dealing with secret filming (*R v Broadcasting Standards Commission ex p. BBC*, 2001) in which he noted that the privacy of a human being denotes at the same time the personal space which should be free from intrusion, namely: 'An infringement of privacy is an affront to the personality, which is damaged by both the violation and by the demonstration that the personal space is not inviolate'.[112]

Subsequently in 2005, the European Court of Human Rights took these arguments a stage further in their consideration of a case brought by Princess Caroline of Monaco (*Von Hannover v Germany*[113] in 2004) who objected to the publication in German magazines of photographs of her going about her normal life in various places.

The German courts had ruled that the princess's children were entitled to protection, but that she as 'a role model' was not, except in a secluded restaurant. But the Strasbourg court identified a 'zone of interaction of a person with others, even in a public context, which may fall within the scope of "private life"' and held that the photographs fell within the scope of her private life.

Moreover, even though she was a public figure, she still had a right to a private life. There had been no public interest in the publication of the pictures and articles as they made 'no contribution to any political or public debate'. The judgment also referred expressly to a positive obligation on the State 'to protect private life and the right to control the use of one's image'.

This is now a key judgment, which is being applied by the Court of Appeal in cases such as that brought by J. K. Rowling against the photographic agency which had taken long-lens pictures of her family out on an Edinburgh street. It tests the right or otherwise for news organisations as well as the paparazzi to take pictures in public places of children and others who are not necessarily engaging in private activity.

Rowling lost her original high court case against Big Pictures who had taken pictures of her 18-month-old son in April 2005. The original trial judge, Mr Justice Patten, in turning down Rowling's arguments said that although he had every sympathy with anyone who wished to shield his or her children from intrusive media attention he did not believe that

---

[112] *R v Broadcasting Standards Commission ex p. BBC*, 2001.
[113] Press release from the Registrar on *Von Hannover v Germany*:
www.echr.coe.int/eng/Press/2004/June/ChamberjudgmentVonHannover240604.htm

the law, in my judgement, allows them to carve out a press-free zone for their children in respect of absolutely everything they choose to do ... If the law is such as to give every adult or child a legitimate expectation of not being photographed without consent on any occasion on which they are not, so to speak, on public business, then it will have created a right for most people to the protection of their image ... If a simple walk down the street qualifies for protection, then it is difficult to see what would not ... For most people who were not public figures, there would be virtually no aspect of their lives which could not be said to be private.[114]

Taking Baroness Hale's point in the Campbell case, he suggested there was 'an area of routine activity which, when conducted in a public place, carries no guarantee of privacy'. But the Court of Appeal subsequently overturned his ruling, as it clearly felt more bound by the Strasbourg decision. Delivering the ruling, the Master of the Rolls, Sir Anthony Clarke, said:

If a child of parents who are not in the public eye could reasonably expect not to have photographs of him published in the media, so too should the child of a famous parent ... In our opinion, it is at least arguable that a child of 'ordinary' parents could reasonably expect that the press would not target him and publish photographs of him.[115]

The full arguments have still not been tested. But we are left with a clear steer that paparazzi activity directed at children is going to fall foul of the law, and that probably quite a lot of pictures of celebrities going about their normal life are also becoming off-limits. Commenting on the case, Hugh Tomlinson QC, an expert on privacy law, has suggested:

In this case an English court has held, for the first time that the publication of an inoffensive photograph of an everyday activity in the street could amount to an invasion of privacy. This brings English privacy law more closely into line with the position in

[114] J. Coad, 'J. K. Rowling Fails to Prevent Publication of her Son's Photograph', *Swan Turton ebulletin*, 9 Aug. 2007: www.swanturton.com/ebulletins/archive/JKCRowlingphotograph.aspx
[115] C. Dyer, 'J. K. Rowling Wins Ban on Photos of her Son', *Guardian*, 8 May 2008: www.guardian.co.uk/media/2008/may/08/privacy.medialaw

France. This case puts in place another building block in the gradual construction by the courts of a fully developed law of privacy.[116]

The danger here is the confusion of different issues. Is what is being addressed the harassment of celebrities or other public figures? Some measurement of protection from being followed through every waking moment is justified.

But the public interest test set out in Von Hannover of 'contribution to political or public debate' is a high hurdle indeed. While it is possible to have sympathy for people whose lives are subject to constant harassment by others seeking to exploit their image for money, there is a balance to be struck between what is reasonable and unreasonable. But is there, or should there be, a privacy right in one's image *per se*? Our faces are not a private matter. We present them to the world every day. Is the real issue here one of copyright and protecting a financial interest in the use that is made of the image?

The Max Mosley case

If the test for a breach of privacy is that of the public interest as opposed to what the public might be interested in, that test was failed effectively by the *News of the World* in the action brought by Max Mosley. Mr Justice Eady (once again) pointed in his judgment to the fact that:

The law now affords protection to information in respect of which there is a reasonable expectation of privacy, even in circumstances where there is no pre-existing relationship giving rise of itself to an enforceable duty of confidence. That is because the law is concerned to prevent the violation of a citizen's autonomy, dignity and self-esteem. It is not simply a matter of 'unaccountable' judges running amok. Parliament enacted the 1998 statute which requires these values to be acknowledged and enforced by the courts.[117]

---

[116] Ibid.
[117] *Mosley v News Group* (July 2008), para. 7. The entire judgment can be found at http://news.bbc.co.uk/1/shared/bsp/hi/pdfs/24_07_08mosleyvnewsgroup.pdf

His judgment neatly encapsulates the approach now taken by the courts:

> *This modern approach of applying an 'intense focus' is thus obviously incompatible with making broad generalisations of the kind to which the media often resorted in the past such as, for example, 'Public figures must expect to have less privacy' or 'People in positions of responsibility must be seen as 'role models' and set us all an example of how to live upstanding lives'. Sometimes factors of this kind may have a legitimate role to play when the 'ultimate balancing exercise' comes to be carried out, but generalisations can never be determinative. In every case 'it all depends' (i.e. upon what is revealed by the intense focus on the individual circumstances) ... The judge will often have to ask whether the intrusion, or perhaps the degree of the intrusion, into the claimant's privacy was proportionate to the public interest supposedly being served by it.*[118]

The point to note is that the balancing process necessarily involves an evaluation of the use to which the right to freedom of expression is to be put. Generally speaking 'political speech' will be accorded greater value than gossip or 'tittle-tattle'. (See also *Campbell* at [148] and also *Jameel v WSJ* [2007] 1 AC 359 at [147].)

Eady concluded on the facts that Max Mosley had a reasonable expectation of privacy in relation to his sexual activities (albeit unconventional) that were carried on between consenting adults on private property. Given that there was no evidence that the gathering was intended to be an enactment of Nazi behaviour, or adoption of any of its attitudes, he saw no genuine basis at all for the suggestion that the participants mocked the victims of the Holocaust.

While there was bondage, beating and domination, there was no public interest or other justification for the secret recording; for the publication of the resulting information and still photographs; or for the placing of the video extracts on the *News of the World* website.

There have been serious objections to Eady's judgment from powerful voices in the press. Lord (William) Rees-Mogg, the former editor of *The Times*, wrote in that newspaper (25 July 2008) that:

---

[118] Ibid., para. 12.

judges are reluctant to accept that newspapers are one of the few remaining safeguards. Journalists more often than lawyers are the people who investigate the more disreputable areas of life. We have recently seen in some very painful cases involving the social services and the family courts that there is far too little exposure of serious injustices in cases that the press is not free to report. Any reduction in the ability of the press to investigate and to publish is likely to have serious consequences against the general welfare of society.[119]

But this defence hardly meets the facts of the Mosley case.

Still more powerfully, Paul Dacre, the editor of the *Daily Mail,* in a speech to the Society of Editors in November 2008, argued that:

Mr Justice Eady ... is ruling that—when it comes to morality— the law in Britain is now effectively neutral, which is why I accuse him, in his judgments, of being 'amoral' ... all this has implications for newspapers and, I would argue, society. Since time immemorial, public shaming has been a vital element in defending the parameters of what are considered acceptable standards of social behaviour, helping to ensure that citizens— rich and poor—adhere to them for the good of the greater community. For hundreds of years, the press has played a role in that process. It has the freedom to identify those who have offended public standards of decency—the very standards its readers believe in—and hold the transgressors up to public condemnation ... if mass circulation newspapers, which also devote significant space to reporting and analysis of public affairs, don't have the freedom to write about scandal, I doubt whether they will retain their mass circulations, with the obvious worrying implications for the democratic process.[120]

The serious point is whether this judgment, and others using the same criteria, will limit journalists' right to investigate matters which they regard as being in the public interest. Dacre appeals to a tradition which has been alive as long as newspapers. In the nineteenth and first half of the twentieth

[119] W. Rees Mogg, 'Mosley Did Not Deserve the Law's Protection', *The Times,* 25 July 2008: www.timesonline.co.uk/tol/comment/columnists/william_rees_mogg/article4392916.ece
[120] Society of Editors: Paul Dacre's speech in full can be found at www.pressgazette.co.uk/story.asp?storycode=42394

century, it was routinely used and caused many casualties among the powerful whose sexual lives, whether adulterous, or homosexual, or more than usually inventive, were, once revealed, judged by their leaders, their electors or themselves to be incompatible with their public position. This tradition is far from exhausted: but the law, and probably society, has moved against it.

As we have seen, the courts have been ready to uphold the public interest in responsible journalism but have started to draw a line around private behaviour that does not impinge on public duty. It is a complicated issue, not least because some journalists see the courts as seeking to involve themselves in editorial matters and that that potentially does indeed have a 'chilling effect' on freedom of information and expression.

Leaving aside the moral arguments, however, what is most likely is that, had the *News of the World* simply published the story without the pictures, and assuming its facts were right, there is unlikely to have been the grounds for an effective challenge. Mr Justice Eady makes great play of the use of the images as going to the heart of the invasion of privacy, much as the House of Lords argued in the Campbell case. An accurate factual report of an orgy without the intrusive images would have been easier for the *News of the World* to defend.

The existing codes

It is now nearly twenty years since the Calcutt Report, which sought to look at whether the press could regulate itself over privacy or whether legislation was needed. The intervening period has seen a refinement of the press code and the arrival of a single regulator for privacy in broadcasting, Ofcom. What, if anything, has that done to improve matters?

The Press Complaints Commission's code of practice—which deals with newspapers—first sets out the individual's right to privacy: 'Everyone is entitled to respect for his or her private and family life, home, health and correspondence, including digital communications. Editors will be expected to justify intrusions into any individual's private life without consent.'[121] It then goes on to look at possible exceptions justified by the public interest: but the Code also reinforces another important consideration: 'There is a public interest in freedom of expression itself.' It goes on: 'Whenever the public interest is invoked, the PCC will require

[121] See www.pcc.org.uk/cop/practice.html

editors to demonstrate fully how the public interest was served.' The Ofcom broadcasting code could almost be an echo:

> *Where broadcasters wish to justify an infringement of privacy ... they should be able to demonstrate why in the particular circumstances of the case ... it is in the public interest ... Examples of public interest would include revealing or detecting crime, protecting public health or safety, exposing misleading claims made by individuals or organisations or disclosing incompetence that affects the public.*[122]

So far, perhaps, so consensual and predictable. But note that neither code attempts a full definition of the public interest. The argument is advanced by example: and examples can go this way and that, sometimes—as we have seen—on very small points of law. (We will return to this in a later chapter.) So it's not surprising that people who are exposed to the public gaze sometimes seem to choose discretion over valour when it comes to complaining or suing: they cannot be sure they will win, and more public attention they can do without.

In deciding to brazen out the ridicule and having his claim tested in court, Max Mosley has provided an important public service. He has provoked a debate, with both old and new elements, on the legal definition of the public interest and of private life. Equally, his appeal to the European Court on the right of reply (under way as this is written) will help clarify another important principle in relation to journalistic behaviour when allegations are made. Should journalists be required to put the allegations to those they accuse before publication?

There are potential risks here to freedom of expression. It is not always helpful to put serious allegations to those being accused as they can use heavy-handed methods to prevent publication or indeed simply run from the jurisdiction. These are significant matters for discussion and debate before the European Court of Human Rights.

Meanwhile Hugh Tomlinson QC and Dan Tench have encapsulated the current approach taken by the English courts in five essential points:[123]

(1) The law will protect information that is 'obviously private' or where there is a reasonable expectation of privacy.

---

[122] See www.ofcom.org.uk/tv/ifi/codes/bcode/
[123] D. Tench and H. Tomlinson, 'Privacy Gets the OK', *Guardian*, 7 May 2007: www.guardian.co.uk/media/2007/may/07/mondaymediasection10

(2) The law will protect potentially private information even if it is false.

(3) The availability of information to others even on obscure websites is no longer decisive.

(4) Publication of private information can be justified in the public interest but that is not the same as what the public is interested in.

(5) Everything depends on context, circumstances and impression.

Conclusion

If everything depends on the facts and the underlying balance to be struck—freedom of expression and information balanced against private rights to privacy or reputation—then where does the public interest lie? This is the nub of both press freedom and responsibility: rights matched by duties, recognised by Parliament through the passage of the Human Rights Act. This is not judge-made law, nor does a single judge, as is sometimes alleged, make decisions without being scrutinized by the higher courts. Interestingly, some of the decisions made by Mr Justice Eady that Paul Dacre complained of were not pursued further by the newspapers in the higher courts.

It is hard to see evidence of the courts creating a 'chilling effect' on responsible journalism exercised in the public interest (we explore this further in Chapter 5). They rightly give great importance to the industry codes; the judgement exercised by the editor; the interest in both providing and receiving information which is more than merely 'newsworthy'; the importance of verification and the reliability of sources; the checking of the facts; the putting of allegations; and the tone of the reporting.

But, ultimately, seeking to balance competing freedoms is never easy. Better by far, though, if those decisions are called correctly in newsrooms or editorial offices in the first instance. The courts are making it clear that they require media responsibility. They have given their steer. They should now be the place of last resort. Sir Christopher Meyer, former chairman of the PCC, neatly summed up the reality—and the challenge—in a 2008 speech:

> *There will never be an absolutely definitive ruling either by the judges or by the PCC that draws a universally applicable line between the private space and the public interest. Of course, the courts and the PCC make their decisions within the framework of their respective case law. But, in the end, it comes down to case-*

by-case; and a degree of subjectivity is unavoidable. That is why privacy cases, whether judged by the courts or the PCC, will be controversial till the end of time ... Every now and again you hear cries and whispers, not a million miles away from the newspaper and magazine industry, that perhaps, after all, a privacy law debated and passed by parliament would be preferable to decisions taken by 'unelected' judges via the 'backdoor'. Well, beware of what you wish for.[124]

---

[124] Speech given by Sir Christopher Meyer at the Manchester Art Gallery, 24 Nov. 2008: www.pcc.org.uk/news/index.html?article=NTM5Nw==?oxid=da2f4c0cd4547eff6a464d74ac15b68f

4. What is the public interest?

We have seen how privacy is now regarded by journalists; how the everyday understanding of what constitutes privacy is changing under the impact of self-revelation television and the internet; and how the law is changing to contain what it sees as the unacceptable intrusions made on people's private lives. It is time to ask: how far can and should privacy be protected from intrusion on the part of journalism? An answer to that question is only possible if we can get to a definition of what should, for journalism, constitute the public interest. And though the phrase is constantly used, it means different things to different people.

Adam Cannon, a lawyer at the *Daily Mail*, argued definitions were unhelpful; it was more of a 'feel' issue[125]—'you knew it when you saw it'. But people see it in quite different ways. Many of the examples we have given throughout this essay are of journalists unmasking private, often sexual, behaviour, and claiming that it is in the public interest (and not just of interest to the public) that this be done. This kind of exposure—the modern equivalent of the revelation of sin punished by the stocks—is a powerful tradition in the press, especially the British press. Often despised by critics, it must be taken seriously.

The revelation of sin

Paul Dacre, editor-in-chief of Mail newspapers, is the strongest public proponent of this view. As the editor who most strongly enshrines the old Fleet Street model of one wholly in charge of the style and message of his paper, he believes that a large task of the popular press is the unmasking of amorality.

[125] Interview, London, 10 Sept. 2008.

We saw this expressed in his speech to the Society of Editors. But he made a further important point. Having underlined that the naming and shaming of sexual transgressors was a vital part of the job of the popular press, he went on—'if mass circulation newspapers, which also devote considerable space to reporting and analysis of public affairs, don't have the freedom to write about scandal, I doubt whether they will retain their mass circulations, with worrying implications for the democratic process'.[126]

This is a telling argument, especially at a time of falling circulations. It is also one wholly familiar to TV channel controllers, who argue that they must retain their mass audiences with popular drama, reality and celebrity shows if they are to keep any of that mass for public service programmes. It's also obviously right, in at least one sense. Human society and human communication rely heavily on gossip as currency for the exchange of information. In every society, stories are told about the doings of others. Sometimes the stories are told with affection, sometimes to make a moral point, and sometimes to do harm. Gossip is an essential ingredient of most everyday conversations. Just as no conversation is without a reference to others, so no newspaper or magazine can survive without some reference to the doings of the rich and famous, the celebrity or the public figure. Media gossip is at one level ordinary conversation writ on a much larger screen in which light and shade mix. Andrew Marr provided a much quoted definition:

> we are perpetually intrigued by the extreme, the gruesome, the outlandish ... so journalists learn to take less extraordinary things and fashion them into words that make them seem like news instead ... journalists reshape real life, cutting away details, simplifying events, improving ordinary speech, sometimes inventing quotes, to create a narrative which will work ... journalism is the industrialisation of gossip.[127]

One of the issues to which we have devoted some space here is that this 'industrialization of gossip' has hugely expanded—both through the collusion that takes place between celebrities, their agents and the media and through the actions of those who reveal large amounts of personal information on social networking sites, from popstars like Lily Allen— who in 2007 wrote emotional blogposts on MySpace complaining how fat

---

[126] Dacre, Society of Editors' speech (see n. 120).
[127] A. Marr, *My Trade: A Short History of British Journalism* (Macmillan, 2004).

and ugly she felt[128]—through unknowns thrust into the public gaze, such as Amanda Knox, to the great majority, whose details circulate among their friends, acquaintances and the browsing curious. The sheer explosion of social networks demonstrates the importance of the personal, the gossipy and the scandalous to human interaction—and with it, the habit of making implicit or explicit moral judgements about the characters revealed to us in whatever medium.

Moreover, both the view that the public interest is served by exposing (im)moral example, and the view that public interest should exclude all private life considerations except those demonstrably linked to public dereliction, cover-up or crime, depend on a conception of shared interests and, in investigative journalism, very often a shared potential outrage. The investigative journalists to whom we spoke—such as Davis, Leigh and John Ware—all had in mind an audience who should be informed about such issues as bribery by British Aerospace, the maltreatment in mental homes or the continued freedom of Irish Republican terrorists known to have committed mass murder—and who should be concerned over the possibility that the state of affairs being examined may be as bad as the reporters claim.

But those who argue that the mass media should play a *moral* role also presume that there is a consensus against certain kinds of behaviour—as Dacre put it, of the details of the Mosley case, 'most people would consider such activities to be perverted, depraved, the very abrogation of civilised behaviour of which the law is supposed to be the safeguard … (the press) has the freedom to identify those who have offended public standards of decency—the very standards its readers believe in—and hold the transgressors up to public condemnation'. Both sides assume a concerned citizen: but the first aims to ensure public virtue, while the second also wishes to police private morality.

The latter is both clearly potentially more popular and more testing. It is more popular because of the 'perpetual intrigue' of others' private behaviour, especially sexual behaviour—and the content it provides for conversation, fantasy and reflection on moral stances, especially one's own. But it is also more testing, because of the difficulty of ensuring that the news organization engaged in such moral police work collects verifiable evidence which will stand the test of a trial—especially now, when, as we've noted, the courts are more concerned to protect privacy than in the past. Further, there is the inevitable question of all moral policemen: what of your own standards? A policeman who upholds the law is compromised

---

[128] E. McIntosh, 'Lily, Wills and the Rest of the World', *Guardian*, 15 May 2007: http://www.guardian.co.uk/commentisfree/2007/may/15/popstarlilyallencries

if he breaks it: the same would apply to a moral policeman. Those who hold public figures to account for their moral failings are themselves public figures—if for no other reason than that they both collect the evidence and at least implicitly judge the individual concerned guilty. They are public figures because they intervene, sometimes mightily, in public affairs by following the route which Dacre, more than any other figure, has mapped out: their argument is that certain kinds of legal private behaviour could and at times should disqualify a man or woman from public office. Thucydides' account of Pericles' funeral oration—'Just as our political life is free and open, so is our day-to-day life in our relations with others ... We are free and tolerant in our private lives; but in public affairs, we keep to the law'—is not their approach.

In the Mosley case, the nature of the behaviour itself (conjoined with the high public position which, the *News of the World* argued, he held) was enough to make the case of moral degradation. Elsewhere, the argument depends often on two related criteria: the fact of being a role model: and the fact of perpetuating a hypocrisy.

For example, pictures of the singer Kate Moss allegedly using cocaine at a recording studio are clearly an example of illegal behaviour: and the interest in publishing them is said to be because she is a role model. This approach also justifies the sagas of self-destruction of stars such as Amy Winehouse or George Michael, and the constant and relentless pursuit of Gary Glitter. It remains a question whether what this does is simply celebrate or condone the behaviour.

> *Hypocrisy was Camilla Wright's justification for many of the exposés on Popbitch—particularly the stories on the Liberal Democrat MPs, Mark Oaten and Simon Hughes. For a period of months in 2004 and early 2005 Oaten, the Liberal Democrat Home Affairs spokesman, had a relationship with a rent boy, possibly involving one other. Oaten had criticised a judge who found himself in a similar predicament, and he had invited the cameras into family breakfast as part of his leadership campaign. Tom Crone whose paper broke the Oaten story, argues that 'If an MP is doing this within 4–500 yards of his home, going around the corner to the local knocking shop, not just for a straight leg-over situation but for this extreme behaviour every three weeks and paying £2,500 a session, do his voters have a right to know? We say absolutely they do and then let them make up their mind.'*[129]

---

[129] Interview, London, 10 Sept. 2008.

The blogger Iain Dale takes a slightly different view: upholding the right of newspapers to pursue hypocrisy, but dissociating that from any implication of executive ability.

> *With a politician, I don't care if he trusses himself up in women's stockings. If he makes a moralistic issue about sex then that's a legitimate area. But does it affect his ability to run a Department if at 9pm on a Sunday evening he is doing things that some people might find rather distasteful? No it doesn't…. Mark Oaten [is] an interesting case where in theory you could argue his activities did not impact on his ability to be good home affairs spokesman. The fact that he was married and consorting with rent boys was obviously hypocritical but I wouldn't argue that means he could not do his job.[130]*

Simon Hughes, another contender for the Lib Dem leadership and whose sexuality had been an open secret for some time, was finally forced to declare that he was bisexual in a 'frank' interview in *The Sun,* which was clearly otherwise going to expose him after he had denied he was homosexual.[131] Yet gay MPs have been an unremarkable feature of British life for some time now and Hughes is a member of the Liberal Democrats—whose watchword is liberality. The character flaw that was held to have mattered was that he dissembled—and that he had won his parliamentary seat in competition, at one time, with the gay rights activist, Peter Tatchell.

Camilla Wright thinks she was right to aid the exposé—although she now displays some unease about what has happened as a result:

> *There's much less reverence [now] and you can say anything about anyone. There's generally a feeling that if you become famous you have no right to privacy. The things you do often have unintended consequences. I think it was right to make coverage more truthful, that with celebrities it is not all about an idealised life. But now the pendulum has swung a long way from that. I don't feel responsible but I have played a part in it.[132]*

---

[130] Interview, London, 9 Sept. 2008.
[131] T. Kavanagh, 'Hughes: I've had Gay Sex', *The Sun,* 26 Jan. 2006:
www.thesun.co.uk/sol/homepage/news/article35699.ece
[132] Interview, London, 7 Oct. 2008.

In Naomi Campbell's case, it was the 'hypocrisy' of denying addiction while attending a treatment centre. The commonest accusation of hypocrisy is if a politician is married and has ever been photographed with or referred to his wife or her husband, or if—as was the case in the John Major government—the party has itself taken a line in support of moral values.

In the case of former Deputy Prime Minister John Prescott, exposed by his lover's disaffected boyfriend over his affair with an aide, the exposure was mixed in with photographs showing him playing croquet at his official country residence, Dorneywood. The adultery was thus conflated with the 'hypocrisy' inherent in a man of working class origin playing a sport associated with the leisured upper classes in a publicly owned country house.

Many of the revelations of the *News of the World*'s 'Fake Sheikh' (Mazher Mahmood) are justified on the basis of hypocrisy—none more obviously so than when Mahmood revealed that Jerry Springer, the US chat show host, had had sex with two women, participants in his show, before it was broadcast—while, during that broadcast, lecturing the women that 'having sex with someone you're mad about is special, it's supposed to be something intimate, something personal … when sex is involved you have to make sure you have at least some feeling with the person with whom you're having sex'.

The effective mixture of reasons for the moral approach are a presumed common agreement on norms of sexual behaviour and private morality together with a perceived public interest in policing these norms through exposure and ridicule. It also suggests an acceptance that public figures are regarded as models for the way in which the large majority of non-public figures live their lives. It requires the pointing up of hypocritical behaviour by public figures who proclaim, or who belong to organisations which proclaim, virtues in conflict with that behaviour. It is bolstered by the argument that this approach also sells newspapers and magazines: that people, for whatever reason, wish to read about the clay feet of the rich and famous—and that this popularity ensures (or has ensured: little is certain in the present newspaper market) the continuance of the popular press.

The classic case is not in the UK—but in the US. The American newspaper market differs markedly from that of the UK—there is, for example, no direct equivalent to the tabloid culture, though the (now declining) *National Inquirer* played something of that role. But the Monica Lewinsky affair of 1997/8 (the sexual affair had lasted from late 1995 to early 1997) put into the public arena an encounter between the White House intern Lewinsky and the then President Bill Clinton which brought together private sexual behaviour and public morality in a dramatic and fascinating way. There was, and has been, no implication that the affair as such breached national security, or had an effect on any other area of public policy or action even if the aftermath of the revelation might have.

The condemnation of the affair, largely but not only from the political right as well as from religious figures and communities, was directed at the President's morals, and the unseemliness of sexual encounters taking place within the White House, and in an annexe to the Oval Office. The issue became a—for a time *the*—major plank of political opposition to Clinton from a right which had, by the late 1990s, lost much of the political impetus it had had in the early part of his presidency. And even on a strict view of a division between private and public, the private became uncontroversially public when, in 1998, President Clinton, if at times more than a little ambiguously, publically denied he had 'sexual relations' with Monica Lewinsky, and when both his wife (now US Secretary of State) Hillary Clinton and his Cabinet members supported him in his denial. That denial—the kind of statement a large number of exposed adulterers are, at least initially, prone to make—then convinced even those editors who felt uneasy trespassing on private concerns that they must give what became massive coverage to the event. Private became public by the public actions and statements of the private adulterer: of course, a frank confession at any stage would also have been huge news, but arguably would have ended the matter more quickly.

In an interview—with the *Daily Mail* (25 June 2004)—Lewinsky said that

> *he could have made it right with the book (Clinton's biography, My Life, 2004), but he hasn't. He is a revisionist of history. He has lied. ... I really didn't expect him to go into detail about our relationship ... But if he had and he'd done it honestly, I wouldn't have minded. ... I did, though, at least expect him to correct the false statements he made when he was trying to protect the Presidency. Instead, he talked about it as though I had laid it all out there for the taking. I was the buffet and he just couldn't resist the dessert.*[133]

[133] From an AP report on *USA Today*: 'Lewinsky: Clinton Lies about Affair in New Book', 25 July 2008: www.usatoday.com/life/books/news/2004-06-25-lewinsky-clinton_x.htm

The Monica Lewinsky revelations were the apogee of the private made public: and made so by a powerful current of opinion and of political organisation in the US which did see sexual behaviour as having a direct bearing on fitness for office. Bill Clinton's tendency to have extra-marital affairs had been well known for many years in Little Rock, the state capital of Arkansas where he had been governor: and it dogged him, through the Gennifer Flowers revelations, through his presidential election bid and into the White House. However, with his wife's support, he was able to sideline the issue: Lewinsky was the revenge of the so-called 'moral majority'. Certainly he was someone a large section of the American people had long suspected of being far too morally loose to be their president (it seemed, after the revelations, that they were not the majority, at least not a stable one: the bulk of those polled on the issue viewed it as a private matter, or at least not one deserving impeachment).

The power of this position is manifold. It connects with notions of sin which—even if now weakly anchored in a religious framework—remain strong, especially when connected with sexual behaviour. It exposes hypocrisy—a demonstration always popular, especially when practised by the powerful and the rich. It is comprehensible: almost everyone understands stories of moral failing. It also plays to our love of Schadenfreude—the joy of witnessing humiliation.

Policing the public space

The iconic revelations which bolster the alternative view of the public interest also concerns a US President, of an older vintage. The Watergate affair, the conclusion of which is 35 years old this year, resulted in the resignation of President Richard Nixon in August 1974, after a two-year struggle to deny or downplay actions which amounted to criminal conspiracy to disrupt opponents' campaigns, illegal wiretapping, bribery and corrupt tax audits. None of this concerned Nixon's private actions (except in the sense that he sought to keep them secret): his life was free of sexual scandals. This stood as an exemplar for later generations of reporters because of its unambiguous public importance—coupled with the story of perseverance and careful detection work undertaken, above all, by the two *Washington Post* reporters, Carl Bernstein and Bob Woodward. In a presentation he gives, the investigative reporter David Leigh pinpoints Woodward and Bernstein as the key role models for his generation of journalists—a large reason why he, and others, chose investigation as his trade. In his book *Flat Earth News*, Nick Davies writes that 'in the year I left university, 1974, Carl Bernstein and Bob Woodward … forced US President Nixon to resign. What an idea! ... I became wholly addicted to the idea of being a reporter … most of all, I would change the world.'[134]

It is this view of the public interest—as the exposure of issues which are unambiguously of a public nature and of public concern—which has become the officially dominant one, as against the popular one. The fact that this is the one now sanctioned by governments, regulators, the judiciary and many in the news media has tended to endow the approach which seeks to reveal sin with—partly ironically—something of a disreputable aura.

This irony was prominently on display when, in response to Dacre's Society of Editor's speech, Mosley wrote in the *Guardian* that

> *They [editors like Dacre] like to claim, for instance, that a celeb's sexual indiscretions should be made public because he or she is 'a role model': an absurd argument when publicity is likely to convince admirers to imitate, not refrain. Or that an activity is criminal: well, inform the police—at least the police would allow the person concerned to offer a defence.*[135]

He went on to turn the charge of hypocrisy against Dacre, saying that

> *Another line is the exposure of hypocrisy—yet when the editor of the Sun, Rebekah Wade, spent a night in police cells after allegedly assaulting her husband, Dacre did not feel the need to draw his readers' attention to the campaign the Sun was then running against domestic violence.*

The investigative journalists to whom we spoke—such as Davies, Leigh and Ware—want both to inform and encourage their audience to share their sense of concern about what it reveals about the health of society.

Many were concerned—as Nick Davies reveals in the quotation from his book (above)—to 'change the world'. Investigative reporters are more often on the left of the political spectrum—sometimes far left—than from the right: a source of conflict, as their critics accuse them of having a

---

[134] N. Davies, *Flat Earth News* (Chatto & Windus, 2008).
[135] M. Mosley, 'My Sex Life is of Interest to No One But This Squalid Industry', *Guardian*, 12 Nov. 2008: www.guardian.co.uk/commentisfree/2008/nov/12/comment-mosley-dacre-press-privacy

political, rather than a journalistic, agenda. But even those whose views might be on the right, or those who profess no political preferences, are in undertaking investigations in the public interest assuming the role of ombudsman on behalf of society as a whole—'changing the world' by revealing abuses in the public sphere, and thus prompting corrective action.

As we can see from the various codes, and from the legislation itself (see box), liberal societies agree with this trend in journalism. Here is another irony: investigative reporters often see themselves as operating as guerrillas against various forms of official armies: yet their actions are, at least in theory, sanctioned by years of officially expressed approval. It is of course the case that reporters often do find official obfuscation, delay, distortion and downright lies when they seek to bring to light something which political or corporate power wishes to disguise: yet it is also the case that their general thrust meets more official approval than at any time in the past. A final, and very sharp, irony: as this official approval is embodied in codes and laws, so the financial crisis in the industry increasingly limits the time and money spent on investigations, especially in newspapers.

UK media codes and guidelines give similar accounts of the public interest

1. The Press Complaints Commission Code sets out in art. 3 the individual's right to privacy: 'Everyone is entitled to respect for his or her private and family life, home, health and correspondence, including digital communications'—then goes on to say that

> *The public interest includes, but is not confined to:*
> * *detecting or exposing crime or serious impropriety*
> * *protecting public health and safety*
> * *preventing the public from being misled by an action or statement of an individual or organisation.*

The Code also reminds us of another important consideration: 'There is a public interest in freedom of expression itself. ... Whenever the public interest is invoked, the PCC will require editors to demonstrate fully how the public interest was served.'

2. The Ofcom broadcasting code in s. 8.1 states:

> *where broadcasters wish to justify an infringement of privacy . . . they should be able to demonstrate why in the particular circumstances of the case . . . it is in the public interest . . . Examples of public interest would include revealing or detecting crime, protecting public health or safety, exposing misleading claims made by individuals or organisations or disclosing incompetence that affects the public.*

3. The BBC's Editorial Guidelines state that

> *The BBC seeks to balance the public interest in freedom of expression with the legitimate expectation of privacy by individuals . . . there is no single definition of public interest, it includes but is not confined to: exposing or detecting crime, exposing significantly anti-social behaviour . . . preventing people from being misled by some statement or action of an individual or organisation . . . disclosing information that allows people to make a significantly more informed decision about matters of public importance.*

4. The Information Commissioner, in March 2007, published suggestions on the public interest*

- *Informing debate on key issues*
- *Promoting accountability and transparency for decisions and public spending*
- *Tackling fraud and corruption*
- *Promoting probity, competition and value for money*
- *Helping people understand and challenge decisions affecting them*

5. The law—as in the Freedom of Information Act, and the Data Protection Act ss. 32 and 55)—also recognises a public interest defence and a journalistic exception where there is 'reasonable belief of acting in the public interest'.

Clearly, these attempts at definition show a good deal of consensus. Clearly too, there is room for a good deal of argument as to what the interest really is, and how far one should trespass on private space to pursue that interest.

*Freedom of Information Act Awareness Guidance No. 3: www.ico.gov.uk/upload/documents/library/freedom_of_information/detailed_specialist_guides/awareness_guidance_3_public_interest_test.pdf

The public interest: a definition

Our own definition of the public interest is unambiguously on the side of those who see it as residing in the arena in which men and women conduct their public business. We believe this to be right for the following reasons.

- In the first place, there is a great public interest in the protection of private life. Everyone, whether public figure or private, needs some private space to withdraw from others in order to develop themselves. It is crucial to our integrity as human beings through preserving a mental and physical balance, maintaining and developing personal relationships, pursuing private interests and nurturing personality. It is in itself a public good. We have seen how much that is now under pressure, even under threat. We have seen how public persons, especially politicians, are now regarded by many journalists—especially the 'new' or 'citizen' journalists—as fair game for any kind of exposure. We have seen how easy it has become to put information, true or false, into common currency, and how hard it is to erase such false information. All of this leads to an experience of privacy, on the part of public people, which is fractured and fragile.

- The malign consequences are threefold. First, some close to the political process suggest that men and women of ability are not presenting themselves for public service because they want to protect aspects of their privacy. Second, that those who come to and remain in public life will take ever greater care to protect what privacy they can—and/or use elements of their private life to bolster their popularity, attract sympathy or slide out of a jam. Third, a media culture which pounces on slips, second thoughts and indiscretions enforces blandness and political correctness—the opposite of what a robust democracy needs.

- Any approach which recognises that the private space is to be, in principle, protected will run the risk of missing concealed scandals which bear on public life. For example, David Blunkett's actions when Home Secretary of covertly seeking to fast track a visa application for the nanny of his lover, was discovered because of the revelation of a private sexual affair. The instance illuminates an obvious tendency— that those in public life, especially in high public office, engaged in such affairs are often tempted to misuse their position and power to conceal the matter, or (as in this case) to assist its continuation. But to argue from this that all potentially compromising private relationships must therefore be investigated for what public misdemeanours they may prompt is not a reasonable posture, if private life is seen as worth defending.

- The public interest in this definition assumes that citizens in a democratic state have an interest in having access to information about the workings of that state, of its institutions and its officials, both elected and appointed. However, the public interest is not confined to the state's institutions, but also to private corporations and to voluntary organisations which—as nearly all do—require the public's trust.

- When an individual holds an office, whether in a public institution (as government) or a private company or voluntary organisation which seeks the public's trust for the statements of intent made, the policies pursued, the actions taken, the services and commodities offered or the campaigns undertaken, it is in the public interest that that individual's public actions in pursuit of these goals be open for inspection, analysis and investigation by the news media.

- But such an individual is to be judged for his/her public acts, not private ones. In this case, 'private' should be taken to mean all issues to do with personal relations, personal communications, beliefs of all kinds, past affiliations—always assuming these are within the law. However much these should appear to others, even to an overwhelming majority, to be deviant, or immoral, or bizarre, the test is always the public statements, policies and above all actions.

- It is recognised that the division between private and public is rarely absolute: the person who believes in flying saucers or is conducting a sado-masochistic relationship may be a council officer or a department store manager. But the first set of beliefs or actions cannot be presumed to inform their behaviours in their job. If, in an investigation, links are shown to exist between the public and the private, then the latter is a legitimate area of inquiry by the news media. But there is no prima facie public interest in ET believers, or in sado-masochists.

We acknowledge that morally driven coverage, and the argument that it is only by doing such exposés that we can sustain a mass popular press, is a serious challenge to this approach to the public interest and private lives. That argument locates one of the central tasks of public issue journalism in the duty to reveal the private squalor under the public magnificence, and appeals to a very old tradition—much older than the 'public matters' approach—of exposing our leaders' feet of clay. Further, it links in to moral and implicitly religious categories which exert powerful, even if often unconscious, feelings of what is right and what is not. It also has the pleasure of enjoying what it professes to abhor.

For this approach is itself rarely wholly free of hypocrisy. The *News of the World* is not a Methodist tract: its revelations are largely skewed towards the doings of the celebrity circuit—whose lives are constructed by press agents, and whose misdemeanours are often part of that construction. The evidence we have gathered from those who work this seam—such as Mark Frith, formerly of *heat* magazine, and Camilla Wright of Popbitch—reveal a world in which an elaborate game is played out between the media and the celebrities—not wholly under the control of either, but with broadly defined rules and ceremonies. But, as Dacre put it in his Society of Editors' speech, 'the opinions of its (*NoW*) readers carry, in a democracy, no less weight than the infinitely smaller readerships of papers like the *Guardian*'.

However, there are also a series of disabling arguments to the moral police approach.

- It is hard to prove a connection between most private behaviour and most public actions. We accept, many times a day, that the public figures we encounter or who have some control over our lives will separate public from private, and we are usually justified in this trust. To hold what some—even most—would regard as sleazy private behaviour as a prima facie reason for investigation and exposure is to fly in the face both of common experience and common sense.
- There is no longer a consensus on what constitutes 'immoral' behaviour, where it is private and legal. Until recently, and even occasionally now, much of the press regarded homosexual relationships of any kind as deviant, and would expose them (much male homosexual behaviour was, to be sure, illegal until the passing of the 1967 Sexual Offences Act: but the pursuit and exposure of homosexuals continued long after that). Since the late 1960s, and in part because of the debates about and resolutions on homosexuality, a wider and more generous view has been taken by most, including most democratic governments, of sexual morals and activity. As we noted, the view of most Americans (even in a country in which religious observance is much higher than in the UK) was that President Clinton's sexual business was his own.

The point is well made by reference to the argument which Lord Devlin, the distinguished jurist, had with Lord Wolfenden on the latter's (permissive) report on homosexual law reform, in 1957. Devlin believed that societies needed shared moral values, which were greater than individual, private judgements. Since, in his view, homosexual acts were outside the pale of shared moral values, the law had to intervene to punish them in order to maintain social cohesion. He argued that 'limits of toleration' were reached when this or that act (including homosexuality) excited popular feelings of 'intolerance, indignation and disgust'. If, for example, the majority believes that homosexuality is 'a vice so abominable that its mere presence is an offence', then the law should aim to end it. This approach, rejected by parliament in 1967, is that to which the 'moral police' side appeals. It is no longer available.

- The role model argument is a thin one. Max Mosley is right to point out that if celebrities and others really are role models, revelation of their behaviour is more likely to stir emulation than distaste—since most such 'role models' are known not to have strict sexual and other models before they become such (indeed, that will often be a reason for them being so). Further, holders of posts like the presidency of Formula One do not function as role models in any moral sense: they make no normative pronouncements outside of their professional duties, and are not held up as people who show others how their lives should be lived.

- Journalists are ill-equipped to be moral police. This is not just because there is little evidence to show that their private behaviour is of a higher quality, in any sense, than those in other professions—though that is one consideration. It is also because they have no training in moral discrimination, nor does the profession have a governing philosophy of moral behaviour to which they can appeal when deciding to 'out' an adulterer, or a homosexual, or one whose sexual tastes may be defined as perverted. Such judgements can indeed be made—most obviously, by the clergy, who rely on religious codes and commandments, which variously both describe and prescribe adultery, homosexuality and sexual perversion. Journalists have no such recourse.

- Hypocrisy is the strongest ground for this argument where a defence can be mounted in terms which the 'public matters' side would understand, and with which it might agree. However, how far a public figure's hypocrisy justifies an intrusion into his or her private life is not something which can be decided in principle—but can only be determined by the intense focus exercised by the courts. We shall return to this in the conclusion of the next and final chapter.

5. Is journalism under threat because of privacy?

Our definition of the public interest leaves a large question for journalists—and for the public. Is there a downside? Will it exercise a chilling effect on investigative journalism—and in doing so, damage the public interest it claims to serve?

Privacy is not a new issue for journalism but its salience is. The dilemmas for investigative reporters in the 1970s and 1980s were less about whether journalists were intruding into people's privacy, than whether journalists were permitted to carry out investigations at all. Roger Bolton, former editor of *Panorama*, *This Week* and responsible for the controversial Thames documentary *Death on the Rock*. who did much work on Northern Ireland, found himself frequently wrestling over whether he could even do interviews:

> *For example, in 1977 we looked at alleged torture in the Castlereagh barracks. We talked to people off the record, we recorded interviews ... we eventually had to refer up over whether it should be broadcast at all. Then in 1979 when I was working on Tonight we interviewed someone from the INLA—a breakaway group from the IRA who had claimed responsibility for the death of Airey Neave. At the time, the INLA was not a proscribed organisation but to get the interview the reporter (David Lomax) and producer had to be blindfolded, taken to a destination, film people with masks on. Afterwards Thatcher sent Special Branch to talk to us ... After that we were not allowed to interview a member*

of a proscribed organisation (before that we could not do so without the permission of the director of news or current affairs) and the guidelines were modified.[136]

That now seems very strange to a later generation which takes both the right to investigate and to publish for granted. We have come a fair distance.

There remain, of course, significant barriers to reporting which go beyond the superficial.

The use of the libel law

In an essay for the *New York Review of Books*[137] in January 2009, the editor of the *Guardian*, Alan Rusbridger, noted that the British laws of libel remain strict, and that 'in the Internet age, the British libel laws can bite you, no matter where you live'. In the article, Rusbridger links two important points, brought together by the *Guardian*'s (inaccurate) reporting of a Tesco tax avoidance scheme. The first of these is this: that to understand and report accurately on much modern business practice, including tax avoidance schemes, is fearsomely hard. Coupled with tough libel laws, this could have the effect of 'chilling' investigations.

In the Tesco investigation, the *Guardian* employed two reporters whom Rusbridger describes as 'award-winning specialists'. Nevertheless, they made a major error and some smaller ones. The major error was to mistake Tesco's strategy to be avoiding corporation tax, rather than Stamp Duty Land Tax. Though chagrined by this (and having published more than one apology, including one which said that 'the article was wrong and should not have been written'), the *Guardian* editor concluded that the mistakes were not the result of malice, but of complexity.

Modern financial complexity, coupled with tough libel laws, had and would, Rusbridger claimed, continue to chill informed and detailed reporting on financial and economic affairs—particularly when conjoined with news organisations' shedding of staff. Tellingly, Rusbridger quotes Dan Bogler, managing editor of the *FT*, as saying that 'unfortunately financial journalists—and the *FT* has better-trained financial journalists than others—don't really understand this stuff, and they join a long list of people that starts with bank regulators, central bank regulators and money managers'.

---

[136] Interview, London, 14 Oct. 2008.
[137] A. Rusbridger, 'A Chill on the *Guardian*', *New York Review of Books*, 56/1, 15 Jan 2009.

In his conclusion, Rusbridger writes that

> *British libel law—with its burden of proof on the defendant,*
> *conditional fee arrangements, the ability of lawyers to ratchet up*
> *eye-watering costs and a still uncertain degree of qualified*
> *privilege protection for 'responsible' journalism—remains a*
> *formidable weapon in the hands of claimants, whether rich*
> *individuals or powerful corporations, before putting journalism*
> *on trial, a more responsible standard of public interest should*
> *surely be applied … whether we are dealing with banks, taxation,*
> *security, religion or climate change, we need more than ever to*
> *find ways of encouraging, not penalizing, news organizations that*
> *try to report matters of the greatest complexity and significance.*[138]

Contracting out

From the late 1980s onwards, television companies, including the BBC, came under pressure to use more independent production companies and to move to more contract working using freelancers rather than permanent established teams.

When Bolton was editing *Panorama*, reporters and producers were expected to deliver four 50-minute films a year—roughly six to eight weeks per programme. That was also true of *This Week* on ITV. However, this was within the luxury of an established team, where an editor would have the chance to shuffle the pack—if a programme needed more time, it could be put back and swapped for another.

But for independent companies working on a tight two-week research, two-week shoot, two-week edit scheme as is common, there is usually no extra time or budget to cope with the unexpected: 'That's why you find that independents who do investigations tend to be one- or two-man bands who want to do a subject because they are passionate about it', says Bolton.

Money and time

Even before recession began biting, there was pressure on both broadcasters and newspapers to reduce a style of journalism seen as doing little for ratings or circulation. Investigations are costly in financial as well as personal terms.

---

[138] Ibid.

Practitioners are pessimistic about their future. Sandy Smith, presently (early 2009) editor of Panorama, for example, identifies money and resource issues, the fact that more organisations and individuals are becoming more savvy and more suspicious, and legal issues such as the Children's Act when it comes to looking at care. David Henshaw adds that, in the new TV environment, it is much harder for investigations to have an impact. The commissioners are not so keen on demanding programmes—but TV itself has less importance in people's lives, especially those of young people.

Newspapers are under intense pressure. Those which had blazed the trail of daily investigative reporting—as the *New York Times* and the *Washington Post*—are facing a financial crisis. Michael Hirschorn wrote in *The Atlantic*, of the newspaper which has defined the concept of a 'paper of record' and which has thrown huge reporting resources at stories of importance—'what if the *New York Times* goes out of business? ... it's certainly plausible. Earnings reports released by the New York Times Company in October (2008) indicate that drastic measures will have to be taken over the next five months, or the paper will default on some $400m in debt. With more than £1bn debt already on the books, only $46m in cash reserves as of October and no clear way to tap into the capital markets (the company's debt was recently reduced to junk status) the paper's future doesn't look good.'[139] The trend continues. There was a loss of $94 million in the first three months of this year.

Pressure from ratings

John Ware, one of the BBC's premier investigative reporters, believes, like Bolton, that the appetite for 'big picture' reporting has waned. As he concedes, there are instances where time and space are still given to investigations: he estimates he was given 'four or five months' to make a half-hour Panorama programme on Omagh in 2008—but this, he says, is unusual. The programme controllers no longer back that kind of programme.

> *With Omagh we did have enough for an hour programme but there was no way the controller wanted that—Ireland just wasn't 'sexy' enough. That was made clear. If we'd had someone from GCHQ confessing on tape, maybe they would have thought about it [giving us an hour]. Well that's just ludicrous.*[140]

---

[139] M. Hirschorn, 'End Times?', *The Atlantic* (Jan./Feb. 2009), 41.
[140] Phone interview, 4 Nov. 2008.

He claims that BBC controllers are no longer steeped in news and current affairs as they once were ('And without news and current affairs the BBC is nothing' he adds) and as a result there is less sense of priority, but it also affects how investigations are done. While, again like Bolton, he acknowledges that technology has made undercover work much easier, the change in the style of investigation has changed more fundamentally:

The 'sexy' bits are what are focused on—the how rather than why—'here's a bad thing, now here's another bad thing' rather than any explanation. When John Birt came in to the BBC he spoke of seeing a 'bias against understanding' and I think we have moved to that sort of thing again.[141]

The codes on undercover reporting

(1) For broadcasters, the approved way to do undercover reporting is effectively set out in the Ofcom Broadcasting Code:

8.13 Surreptitious filming or recording should only be used where it is warranted. Normally, it will only be warranted if:

- *there is prima facie evidence of a story in the public interest; and there are reasonable grounds to suspect that further material evidence could be obtained; and it is necessary to the credibility and authenticity of the programme.*

Through its adjudications, Ofcom makes it clear that it expects broadcasters to be able to justify their decision to infringe privacy by reference to the public interest that is involved, that they do not engage in fishing expeditions, and that they can demonstrate a very clear audit trail both in relation to the decision to record as well as broadcast.

(2) On 'privacy and subterfuge', the Press Complaints Commission Code of Practice for newspapers states:

3 Privacy
i)   ... Editors will be expected to justify intrusions into any individual's private life without consent.

ii)   It is unacceptable to photograph individuals in a private place without their consent. Note—Private places are public or private property where there is a reasonable expectation of privacy. ...

10 Clandestine devices and subterfuge
i)   The press must not seek to obtain or publish material acquired by using hidden cameras or clandestine listening devices; or by intercepting private or mobile telephone calls, messages or emails; or by the unauthorised removal of documents or photographs; or by accessing digitally-held private information without consent.

ii)   Engaging in misrepresentation or subterfuge, including by agents or intermediaries, can generally be justified only in the public interest and then only when the material cannot be obtained by other means.

---

[141] Phone interview, 4 Nov. 2008.

These are very large woes, with which journalism is presently burdened. But it does not seem that a 'chilling' effect from curbs on intrusion into privacy is among them—at least, not in public interest journalism as we have defined it. The point is made in the story of a major—and very intrusive—investigation, in the form of the BBC programme, *The Secret Policeman.*

In early 2003, a young BBC journalist, Mark Daly, started as a new recruit at the police academy in the North-West which trains officers for the Greater Manchester, North Wales, Cheshire and Lancashire forces. Nine months later, his report, *The Secret Policeman,* caused a public outcry, brought about significant change in police recruitment and training, and won a number of major broadcasting awards.

It could have gone very wrong. To place an undercover journalist inside the police service to investigate whether it was maintaining a culture of racism was itself an audacious act: the potential difficulties ranged from wasting police time and possibly endangering the public, to whether any arrests in which he participated could be challenged as unlawful. It was an act described at the time by a senior Home Office official, in a letter to the BBC just before transmission in which he sought to get the programme cancelled, as 'the sort of behaviour that might be relevant to a Third World dictatorship rather than Britain'.

The prompt for the programme came when the programme makers came across a number of internal Greater Manchester Police documents and reports that suggested that the tag of 'institutional racism' could still be applied to the GMP. Added to that were available figures on the recruitment and retention of ethnic minority police in the force, plus evidence from officers—all of which suggested that there could be a culture which discriminated against recruits from ethnic minority backgrounds.

That was the prima facie evidence the BBC considered justified further investigation. But simply seeking to discover the facts on the ground from outside of the force would not get close enough to the reality. Would it be possible to get a journalist in a position where he could see for himself what was actually going on inside? Eventually a decision was taken at the top of the BBC to go ahead, provided the right person could be found and the investigation conducted as fairly, and robustly, as possible.

Mark Daly's rules of engagement were clear: he was not to act as an agent provocateur, nor must he use alcohol or any other means to lower the guard of his colleagues. He could only record conversations or classroom scenes once it had become clear that he was dealing with racist attitudes or behaviours. His objective was get beyond the training school and 'on to the beat' so as to find out at first hand what was actually going on.

He survived for over six months within the GMP and did get on to the beat, briefly, before he was finally detected, arrested and then released without charge. The footage he shot of officers-to-be, whose racism had not been detected at the recruitment stage and which was not effectively challenged within the training process, produced widespread shock. The film showed one fellow recruit, in particular, making a Ku Klux Klan headdress; revealed the casual racism of many conversations and the intent of some to arrest people, as soon as they were able, on the basis of colour rather than crime. But these incidents were all carefully considered before Daly could record them, as he recalls:

> *I had to find prima facie evidence about an individual before I could even switch on my camera. I would have to spend time with these people, keep contemporaneous notes, videos, diaries and present this to editorial policy saying 'this is what I have discovered about Officer A' so they could say 'yes go ahead'.*
>
> *I was never allowed to be racist or made racist comments. All I was allowed to do was acquiesce, laugh at jokes ... for example there was an Asian guy in our class and I could say something like 'what do you think of [him]?' which could ignite things.*[142]

In the process, Daly filmed secretly in classrooms, cars and in his study bedroom. Numbers of people were identifiable. There were decisions to make about who should be identified in the film and what was the justification for their inclusion. In the end, those judgments were made on the basis of who had displayed blatantly racist attitudes or behaviour. Action was also taken to protect the identity of the fellow recruit who had been their victim.

The investigation provides a template for modern-day reporting. It followed a clear path: first, prima facie evidence of significant public interest that justified the decision to investigate further by going undercover, as well as the potential intrusion into privacy that flowed from it. A clear set of rules by which any decision was taken to record secretly, with those decisions clearly recorded and the content of the recording logged as soon as possible after the event, together with a contemporaneous diary of events kept by Daly. There was also a second and later decision about what to broadcast of what was recorded and whether identities needed to be protected. Lastly, as part of the editing

[142] Phone interview, 12 Nov. 2008.

process, someone completely unconnected with the process tested every edit and the context for each sequence to be sure that the case was not overstated and that those featured were being treated fairly.

The stakes were particularly high: the programme was being prepared while the BBC was under examination by Lord Hutton, for having claimed that a dossier published by the government contained deliberate lies about Iraq's weapons. It was widely believed that this, and Hutton's judgment that the BBC bore the prime responsibility for the episode, would curb its investigative zeal. In fact, the programme—though bitterly resented by the police and the Home Office—was broadcast, and caused a major scandal. Its success showed others what could be done with the technique—presuming that the issue carried a strong public interest.

There were and remain large problems: but they lie more in the domain of operational journalism than in any official or judicial 'chilling'. Among the most significant was how to deal with the difficult privacy issues, the personal dilemmas that resulted from Mark Daly's role as a journalist and the tension that imposed with regard to his relationships with the subjects of the investigation—relationships forged over a period of intense living together. As Daly says:

> I was living with these guys for seven months and always in the back of my head I knew for want of a better word I could end up f***ing up their lives and their jobs. I felt often it wasn't fair battle—I was educated compared with these guys who had a poor education, who had been exposed to racism at home and I knew this was going to hurt.[143]

These are difficult ethical decisions for anyone involved in such programmes. David Henshaw of Hard Cash productions has made a number of investigative programmes over the years:

> Investigations are complex, time consuming and require much time and support. The reporters require backup and TLC, not least because they are usually having to demonstrate that they can do the job they are investigating to the best of their ability while making the film. It can lead to tensions and difficulties as you are going to be shopping the people with whom you have established a relationship.[144]

---

[143] Phone interview, 12 Nov. 2008.
[144] Interview, London, 24 Sept. 2008.

As well as the relationships built up, the investigative journalist also has to make hard decisions about who to identify. In an *Undercover Mosque* programme, Henshaw's reporter, herself a Muslim woman, secretly filmed two extremist female preachers at the Regent's Park mosque. As usual before transmission, Hard Cash had written setting out the evidence and asking for comment. One of the women asked if her face could be blurred because she feared she would be in danger. Henshaw decided not to take the risk of compromising her security, as it would be too easy to blame the programme if anything happened to the woman. The point was to identify what was happening, not her *per se*.

It is equally a challenge when dealing with whistleblowers whose identity must be protected. The internet allows a report to be viewed anywhere, at any time. Attention has to be paid, therefore, to protecting identities of people exposed in vulnerable situations—as, for example, children shown in slave or indentured labour sweat shops in the developing world.

Sandy Smith of *Panorama* also points to whether or not it is appropriate to finger people who are the victims of the policy rather than its architects. For example, in a report on poor health care:

> You first place a reporter undercover to discover whether there was something to pursue. If that suggested there was a case to answer, then would come undercover secret recording. But that is when the dilemmas begin. Basically, any reporter would be seeing the impact of decisions made in the board room or higher management offices. Who is to blame if too many mothers are being looked after by too few people? The midwives are the ones under pressure, perhaps swearing or apparently not caring enough. Should they be identified in the programme? They are the little people taking the rap for the failures of the system. Who to blob (i.e. disguise) becomes a real challenge.[145]

Yet, as their concerns make clear, these are matters which programme makers work out according to ethical codes which their organizations observe, or have themselves created: a strong contrast with the fear of government censorship which Roger Bolton described in the 1970s and 1980s.

---

[145] Interview, London, 10 Sept. 2008.

Seeking to get to the bottom of what is happening behind closed doors often requires some degree of deception. If, as David Leigh suggests, somewhere in all of this is the price we pay for liberty then we need to be clear about the challenges. Leigh argues that deception should only happen if there is no other way of getting the information. But just as broadcasters have become increasingly entranced with 'secret filming', so he feels print investigators have turned to the 'sting' or subterfuge as a first rather than last resort. Of 120 stories he did about BAE over five years, he said that only one had been a sting (in collaboration with a Swedish TV company).

> *The whole business of developing technology has made stings so easy to do that people now sit around thinking 'what can we do an undercover sting on?' rather than 'what do we need to expose?' I'm not a nun, I'm a practitioner, I'm willing to get down in gutter if necessary—but only if necessary. And a good guideline is only do this if you've tried everything else and it hasn't worked. Journalism is supposed to be about truth—it's very funny then if what you are doing is telling lies routinely.*[146]

Press and broadcasters: different approaches

Broadcasters in the main felt that the way in which they are regulated meant it was much harder for them to breach privacy than for newspapers as much more had to be justified. As Chris Wesson of ITV puts it:

> *For a newspaper it is a commercial consideration; how much is this story worth?—weighing up the possible revenue against the cost of any possible legal claim. For the broadcaster there is the blessing and curse of regulation and a greater regard for bread-and-butter privacy issues. It is also a different commercial model. TV is also not as interested in celebrity tittle-tattle and tends to be more reactive to it.*[147]

He also believes that broadcasters are obliged to take the complaints of the non-powerful more seriously and that Ofcom takes a tougher line than the PCC. Celebrities go to the courts; the individual goes to the regulator.

---

[146] Interview, London, 4 Nov. 2008.
[147] Interview, London, 14 July 2008.

Chris Loweth of Channel Five points to the fact that broadcasters also have to draw a distinction between the decision to gather material and the decision to broadcast, while Kevin Marsh of the BBC College of Journalism was very clear that 'fishing trips' were forbidden.

The problem of 'fishing trips' has been brought to the fore with the Information Commissioner's detailing of the 305 journalists who he believes paid illegally for private and personal data using private detectives and other intermediaries. Leigh refers to this as the 'dark side of journalism'. He said that what was revealed about (Clive) Goodman's misdemeanours was 'less significant than they had this private dick on the payroll for £100k a year. That's what bothered me.'

> *The big problem I have is with intrusive methods. Just as I'm in a bit of minority at the Guardian, in that I think we should take a far tougher line on people's sex lives, so I am also in minority in Fleet St in my opposition to intrusive methods. In my experience, the use of private detectives is increasing; it's unjustifiable and it ought to be stopped ... the Information Commissioner proposals got knocked back because the Mail et al. went and lobbied Gordon Brown who doesn't want the papers against him with a looming election. So the whole debate has been corrupted, it's all been politically tainted.*[148]

The challenge here is less the nature of the process, than the newspapers' traditional reluctance to come under close scrutiny from any outside body, especially statutory. Yet their increased web presence is decreasingly distinguishable from (statutorily regulated) broadcasters: and the trend of the law and of prevailing opinion presently favours transparency and accountability. Since newspapers lead that charge, their own reluctance becomes less easy to defend.

In her Reith lectures on Trust in 2002, Onora O'Neill had some tough things to say about the press. Her central thesis was a free press had to be accountable. Press freedom has to be used to enable the public to explore and test opinions and 'to judge for themselves *whom* and *what* to trust' and that in turn depends on accountability: 'Real accountability provides substantive and knowledgeable independent judgment of an institution's or professional's work.'[149] Assessability is as important as accessibility.

---

[148] Interview, London, 4 Nov. 2008.
[149] The text of O'Neill's Reith lecture on press freedom can be found at www.bbc.co.uk/radio4/reith2002/lecture5.shtml

Conclusion

Undercover techniques are also available to those who wish to reveal wrongdoing: indeed, they are more frequently used in such situations. The 'Fake Sheikh' is, after all, an elaborate deception mechanism. Mahmood, once named forty-fifth most powerful man in Britain, notes in his book's introduction that

> *Subterfuge is a legitimate and basic tool of investigative journalism and the Fake Sheik is just one of a whole range of personas that I adopt to infiltrate targets ... Without going undercover I would have no hope of exposing drug dealers, paedophiles and the like. After all, no one would offer to sell me drugs or weapons if I proudly announced I am a reporter from the News of the World.*[150]

Mahmood's investigations, the most famous and high profile of any reporter in recent years, are a mixture. Some, like the revelations of the private lives of the supermodel Sophie Anderton, or the former Cabinet minister David Mellor, or the Football Association secretary Faria Alam, are pure sex tales. Others, like the unmasking of the would-be murderer Dr Manohar Rangwani, are clearly in the public interest. Still others, like the hypocrisy of Jerry Springer—denouncing casual sex on TV to the women with whom he had just had casual sex—are in the boundary between the two, the revelation justified by the crass hypocrisy of a very public person.

That boundary should remain, even if (necessarily) fuzzy. It is the area within which we decide—through regulators, judges and through the ethical stance which journalists themselves take—how far we legitimize journalism to probe into secrets. Our belief is that the duty and the privilege of undertaking such investigations, essential to the maintenance of a democratic polity, must be vigorous in the pursuit of public understanding—and understanding of the necessity for a private life.

---

[150] M. Mahmood, *Confessions of a Fake Sheik: The King of Sting Reveals All* (Harper Collins, 2008).

Conclusions

Paradoxes and challenges

The contemporary contemplation of privacy; its place in what we might hope is an open but also a humane society; and what justifies its exposure to the public space presents us with a series of paradoxes and challenges.

It starts with the definition of privacy itself. US Supreme Court Justice, Louis Brandeis, coined the phrase: 'the right to be left alone'.[151] Robert Ellis Smith, editor of the *Privacy Journal*, goes further. He suggests that privacy is 'the desire by each of us for physical space where we can be free of interruption, intrusion, embarrassment, or accountability and the attempt to control the time and manner of disclosures of personal information about ourselves'.[152] As Bradwell and Gallagher put it in the Demos publication *UK Confidential*:

> *Privacy still matters because it provides the space to withdraw from the gaze of others and to rest from the need to perform socially. Moreover it matters politically and democratically because it is intimately connected with how we are seen, represented and treated by the people, organisations and institutions that hold influence and power over us.*[153]

If once we saw the threat to privacy as essentially coming from the State, increasingly the media is seen to be as threatening by means of its power and intrusive techniques. The Calcutt Committee, set up in the UK government in 1990 specifically to look into press behaviour and privacy,

---

[151] Samuel Warren and Louis Brandeis, 'The Right to Privacy', *Harvard Law Review*, 4 (1890), 193–220.
[152] www.privacyinternational.org/article.shtml?cmd[347]=x-347-559062.
[153] Edwards and Fieschi, *UK Confidential*, 70–1.

came up with a potential legal definition: 'the right of the individual to be protected against intrusion into his personal life or affairs, or those of his family, by direct physical means or by publication of information'.[154]

We need a free media that can expose wrongdoing and challenge those in power but, if the media is going to infringe privacy, it needs to take care that it is standing on the firm ground of public interest and that the means it employs to investigate are not fatally compromised either by the wrong choice of target or the manner in which the investigation is conducted.

Key findings

In the course of this report we have looked at the tensions that exist between public and private life and come to a number of key findings:

- Everyone whether public figure or private needs a private space to withdraw from others in order to develop themselves. It is crucial to our integrity as human beings through preserving a mental and physical balance, maintaining and developing personal relationships, pursuing private interests and nurturing personality

- For some, though, privacy has become a commodity: the already famous seek to extend their fame through publicity and controlling both image and access for money or favours; for unknowns as a means to gain access to fame and fortune.

- The internet has begun to change our perception of privacy both because social networking and other sites are places where hitherto private information is exchanged between 'friends'—not always with thought for the consequences and because rumours and innuendo spread more quickly.

- Sex, sexuality, health, family life, personal correspondence and finance (except where public monies are involved or reveals wrongdoing or corruption) are all seen as areas that should not be exposed without a significant public interest justification. We expect to have the highest protection of privacy around what happens in the home, in hospitals or other areas of health care, or places where people are at their most vulnerable.

[154] *Report of the Committee on Privacy and Related Matters* (Cm. 1102, HMSO, 1990).

- The greatest differences arise over who should have a right to privacy. Children and ordinary citizens are felt to have higher rights to privacy than celebrities and public figures, although that is being placed under strain by developments on the internet; can people who post intimate details about their life on the web have the same expectations of privacy?

- Most journalists are very comfortable with the idea that, if someone has put themselves into the public domain, then they can expect to have their private life scrutinised. But as at least one political blogger points out: 'That puts a lot of people going off into political and public life. Why put your family through that agony? We are missing out whole range of people—we'll never have another Churchill or Lloyd George—imagine them today. We are getting little personalities with little experience of life—and I'm not sure politics is the better for it.'

- Before seeking to infringe privacy, journalists need to consider an impact test: are they exposing issues which have the potential to impact on the lives of a number of people rather than simply be interesting to the prurient? But restrictions on resources, time and presumed public indifference are what are constraining investigations, not fear of infringing privacy

- There is no evidence of the courts exercising a 'chilling' effect on responsible journalism in the public interest but there is a challenge for newspapers and magazines who build a business model solely on infringing privacy through intrusive photographs or 'kiss and tell' revelations.

- As a result of media excess, the courts are increasingly being used to test the point at which expectations of privacy are trumped by possible public interest in exposure or freedom of expression. Everything depends on the facts and the underlying balance to be struck: freedom of expression and information balanced against private rights to privacy or reputation. On which side does the public interest lie?

- Seeking to balance competing freedoms can never be easy. Better by far, though, if those decisions are called correctly in newsrooms or editorial offices in the first instance. The courts are making it clear that they require media responsibility. They have given their steer. They should now be the place of last resort.

Recommendations

We therefore argue that media investigations have to be proportionate to what is being investigated and clearly targeted. That implies:

- a clear sense of what the public interest justification might be;
- the possession of some justifying evidence to take an investigation forward so that it is not a 'fishing expedition';
- the minimum amount of deception to achieve it;
- very clear rules about when secret recording takes place;
- a clear set of authorisations from within the editorial line management chain;
- a robust rationale for what is eventually put into the public domain and how.

The Press Complaints Commission Code of Practice is clear in both affirming the right to respect for private life and the requirement any intrusion has to be justified. Indeed, it begs the question that, if the code is as clear as it is, how come there are so many disputes over how newspapers behave in practice. The Ofcom code goes further than the PCC by making clear the requirement for prima facie evidence and the two-stage process: first, justify the intrusion, second, defend putting the material in the public domain.

Such an approach is clear, transparent and accountable. Those who work in broadcast journalism cannot point to any example where they suggest the process has damaged investigations conducted in the public interest. We would argue that the same rules should apply to print journalism. Newspapers may quarrel with that, not least because of differing views of what might constitute public interest in a celebrity culture and for commercial reasons. The hesitation is understandable but in a world that is much keener on transparency and accountability (and newspapers lead that charge) their own reluctance becomes less easy to defend.

Investigations are obviously an important way of uncovering matters of public interest ranging from the state of hospital waiting lists, maladministration, corruption, the misuse of public funds, the reality of tax credits or welfare payments, and the state of anti-social behaviour to the questionable activities of estate agents or other professionals. Any public interest justification will include:

- exposing or detecting crime or significantly anti-social behaviour;
- preventing people from being misled by some statement or action of an individual or organisation;
- disclosing information that allows people to make a significantly more informed decision about matters of public importance or incompetence that affects the public;
- informing debate on key issues;
- promoting accountability and transparency for decisions and public spending;
- tackling fraud and corruption;
- promoting probity, competition and value for money;
- helping people understand and challenge decisions that affect them.

The public interest defined

A robust definition of the public interest is possible, and indeed is implicit in the codes, statements and legislation. It has the following main characteristics.

- Citizens in a democratic state have an interest in having access to information about the workings of that state, of its institutions and its officials, both elected and appointed. This interest, however, is not confined to the state's institutions, but also to private corporations and to voluntary organisations which require the public's trust.

- When an individual holds an office, whether in a public institution or a private company or voluntary organisation which seeks the public's trust, it is in the public interest that that individual's public actions in pursuit of these goals be open for inspection, analysis and investigation by the news media.

- Such an individual is to be judged for his/her public acts, not private ones. In this case, 'private' should be taken to mean issues to do with personal relations, personal communications, beliefs and past affiliations—always assuming these are within the law—however much these might appear to others, even to a majority, to be deviant, or immoral, or bizarre. The test is always public actions.

- The division between private and public is rarely absolute: the person who believes in flying saucers or is conducting a sado-masochistic relationship may be a council officer or a department store manager. But the first set of beliefs or actions cannot be presumed to inform their behaviours in their job. If, in an investigation, links are shown to exist between the public and the private, then the latter is a legitimate area of inquiry by the news media. But there is no prima facie public interest in ET believers, or in sado-masochists.

Any approach which recognises that the private space is to be, in principle, protected will run the risk of missing concealed scandals which bear on public life. But to argue from this that therefore all potentially compromising private relationships must therefore be investigated for whatever public misdemeanours they may prompt is not a reasonable posture. There is a greater public interest in the protection of private life: and that interest must tolerate the occasional missed misdemeanour.

When it comes to applying the public interest test, having a clear process in place should ensure that the impact test is taken into account from the outset and that what is done is proportionate to the story.

All those who have suffered from intrusion attest to the scars which it can leave, often more for the family of the public person than for the person him/herself. Public people, especially politicians, are aware that this is a price they may have to pay and develop defence mechanisms. There will be times when the public interest, as defined above, demands it. But it has to be justified by a higher public good. The assumption that a private life is to be protected is itself a considerable and humane public good.

Acknowledgements

We would like to thank all those who contributed their time and insights and experience in the interviews they gave us as part of our research. We, of course, are responsible for any errors and the arguments we put forward in our conclusions.

We would especially like to thank the Reuters Institute for making this study possible and, in particular, John Lloyd for his constant enthusiasm, constructive criticism and assistance in shaping the final report.